PSYCHIC DETECTIVES

PSYCHIC DETECTIVES

The investigators and spies who use paranormal powers

Sarah Moran

Foreword by Marcello Truzzi

Director of the Center for Scientific Anomalies Research

Bramley Books

5152 Psychic Detectives
Published in 1999 by Bramley Books, an imprint of
Quadrillion Publishing Ltd,
Godalming Business Centre, Woolsack Way,
Godalming, Surrey GU7 1XW, England

ISBN 1-84100-239-9

Printed and bound in Italy by G. Canale & C. Spa
Colour reproduction by DP Reprographics Limited,
Wiltshire, England.

CREDITS
Project Manager • Suzanne Evins
Design • Mark Holt
Picture Research • Tony Moore
Copy-editor • Beverly LeBlanc
Index • Peter Dale
Editorial Director • Will Steeds
Art Director • Philip Chidlow

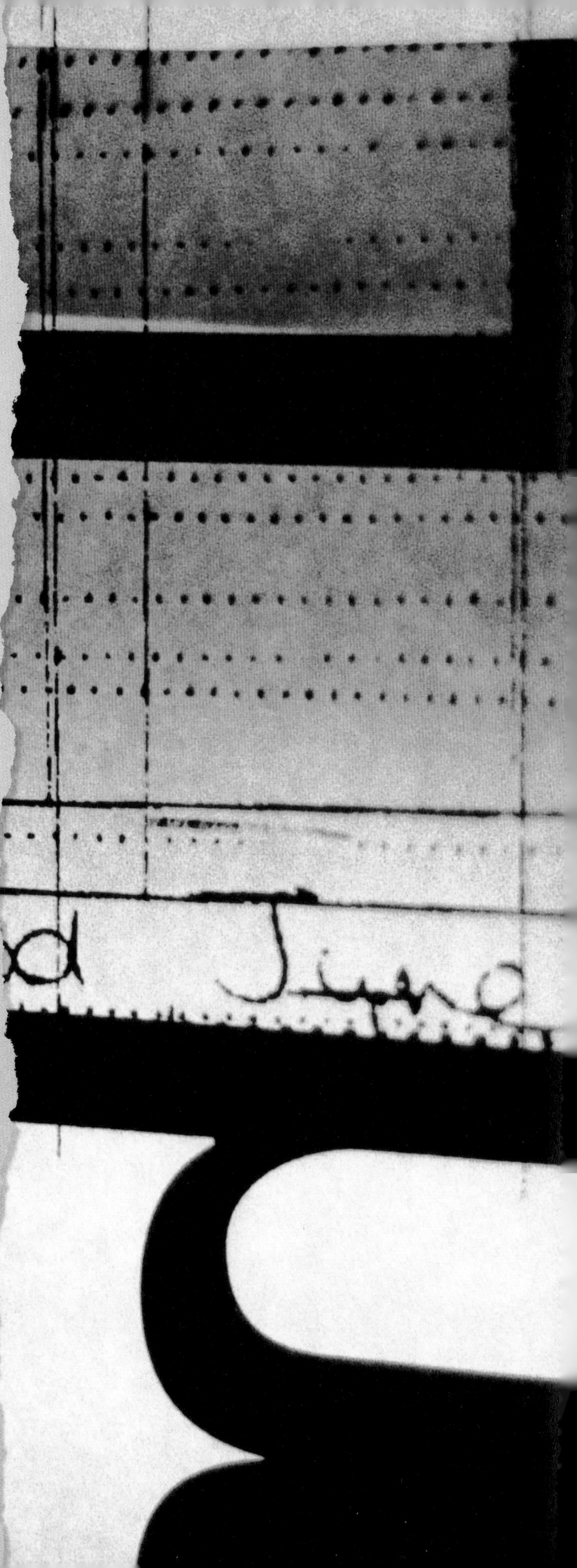

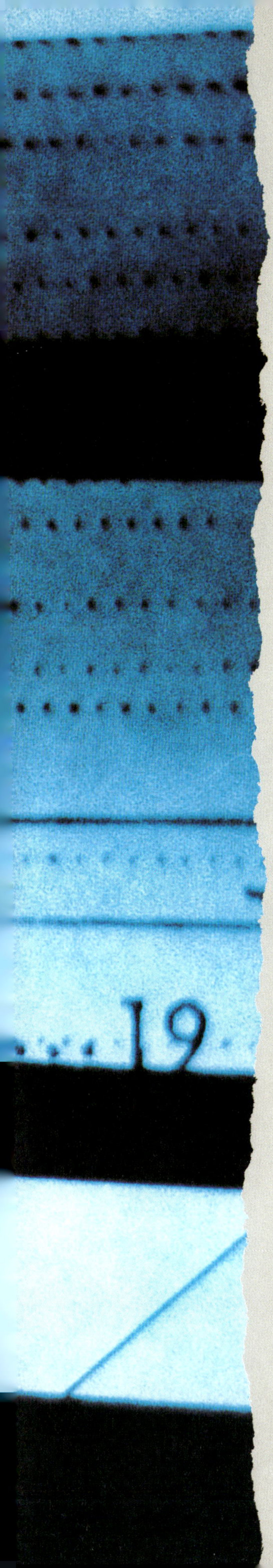

Contents

Foreword

Public opinion polls show that the majority of people believe in extrasensory perception, and surveys taken indicate that those in law enforcement are no more likely to be skeptics. Some police officers have even given a name to their job-related intuitions: the "blue sense." Like most of us, police are no strangers to hunches and gut-feelings, and these have sometimes resulted in saving lives.

The pressures and uncertainties of police work are likely to lead to a willingness to try nonrational as well as rational methods for solutions. Pressures to solve crimes (and sometimes the public's demands can verge on hysteria) are often immense, and we expect our police to "leave no stone unturned." Such demands frequently result in the police trying unorthodox methods, including the use of alleged psychics. In fact, a survey conducted by skeptics in 1993 showed that thirty-seven percent of urban police departments in the United States had on some occasion tried using a psychic. This high figure is all the more remarkable when one considers that psychics mainly work with rural departments, where there are less bureaucratic obstacles to their employment.

Criminal investigation remains largely an art as well as a science. Police today use a wide variety of techniques, including psychiatric profiling, polygraphs, and hypnosis, all of which are scientifically controversial. Since their primary job is solving and stopping crimes, police concern is with practical matters, finding things that work, that help them get the job done. Good cops are pragmatists not laboratory scientists. So they are often willing to try even what some view as outrageous things, if they believe these methods might help resolve a case. While most scientists worry about making the mistake of thinking something works when it really does not, police trying to crack a difficult case cannot afford to miss something rare or unlikely that may be the crucial key to the solution. Part of the business of crime fighting includes the need to sometimes try long shots.

Police recognize that critics of the use of psychics abound. Ironically, such critics are found among both so-called "rationalists" who scoff at all psychic claims as being superstitious nonsense, and among religious fundamentalists who view anything psychic as associated with the occult and the work of Satan. Awareness of such potential criticism, results in much police use of psychics going unpublicized—and even covert. This reaction of secrecy to avoid what has been called the "guffaw factor" has made it particularly difficult to study the subject objectively, for police often are reluctant to make public either their successes or failures with psychics. They know that if their use of a psychic fails, scoffers will ridicule them for being "unscientific"; but if it succeeds, religious fundamentalists will complain about using "the powers of Darkness." It is a Catch-22 situation.

All this is complicated by the problem of what psychics might be credible. There are tens of thousands of people who believe they have had psychic insights into police cases. When a major case is reported in the press (such as the famed 1980 Atlanta, Georgia, child killings), it is not unusual for the police to receive hundreds of (often quite contradictory) communications from "psychics" offering their solutions or help. Simply sifting through all this can be a major administrative problem for a department. If approached by the police, some of these psychics seek publicity, give press interviews, and may give the police a difficult time controlling their own investigation. This is one reason why police usually prefer to contact only the most cooperative psychics, who have been endorsed and quietly referred to them by another police department.

In researching psychic sleuths, we have found it important to recognize that two quite separate issues are involved. One is *validity*, whether or not the psychic powers are real, and the other is *utility*, whether or not the use of psychics is helpful. Most students of the subject have been preoccupied by the former, and their conclusions largely stem from their general orientation towards whether extrasensory perception is a real phenomenon at all. It is probably rationally impossible to reach a strictly scientific conclusion on the matter of validity, because we have inadequate hard data about the rates of failure versus success. Certainly, the best experimental studies conducted (as for example, those by Richard Wiseman) have produced negative results, but that may be a result of the psychic subjects used, or it may be that the phenomena are largely spontaneous and dependent upon naturalistic field conditions. Just as ethologists find animals are known to do some things in the wild that they will not do in labs or zoos, so may psychics best perform under less controlled conditions. Meanwhile, the best thing for police departments to do is probably base their decisions on whether or not to heed a psychic on commonsense grounds, comparing costs and benefits. If a psychic with a good track record suggests one simply look behind a bush for the murder weapon, it costs little to look, and only the most dogmatic scoffer would refuse to peek. Police just need to weigh matters sensibly, the same as they would do with the statements of any other alleged "witness." Open-mindedness does not necessarily mean gullibility.

Despite our inability to draw a final conclusion about the validity of psychic sleuths, there is substantial evidence in favor of their utility. They perform many useful functions, not only for the police but for families and others concerned with the cases—in fact, they can be useful even if quite invalid. To cite just one example, psychics, like polygraphs, have sometimes been used by police to provoke suspects into giving confessions. And psychics often perform quasi-therapeutic functions for relatives of the victims, much like grief counselors. Surely, there are horror stories of expensive psychic failures, but orthodox practices have also led to some catastrophes. Sherlock Holmes lectured Dr. Watson that it is usually a mistake to engage in theory without adequate data. Sarah Moran here nicely provides you with much of the best data that we do have.

Marcello Truzzi, Ph.D., Director of the Center for Scientific Anomalies Research and its "Psychic Sleuths Project"

Introduction

Most of us probably find it easier to believe in the existence of extraterrestrials than in the ability of so-called psychics to predict our futures. Despite this, some people are sufficiently intrigued to at least try a sitting with a clairvoyant, or to respond to one of the hundreds of advertisements for telephone readings that are found in magazines.

The lack of verifying scientific research into the area of psychic ability means very few people are able to grasp how or why it works. While it is true no-one has proved equivocally that psychics' claims are genuine, it is equally true no-one has proved the so-called sixth sense of psychics is all an elaborate hoax, or at least superstitious delusion.

The idea that humans may have another sense, apart from the recognized five (sight, sound, smell, taste, and touch), is a strange one that seems to contradict all that we know about ourselves and how our bodies and minds function. Yet, this potential sixth sense could be the key to unlocking many mysteries currently regarded as paranormal.

Extrasensory perception, or ESP, is a term used to encompass several "paranormal" skills psychics claim to possess. It simply means being able to sense things using abilities other than the five recognized senses. ESP skills can generally be split into three areas of study: Telepathy, where the psychic can allegedly tune into the thoughts, feelings, and emotions of another person; clairvoyance, where the psychic can gain information about a situation or an environment they cannot see; and precognition, the ability to predict what is going to happen in the future. The term psi (which stands for psychical) is also often used to describe the above abilities.

One additional skill sometimes accompanies these other alleged manifestations of the elusive sixth sense, that of psychokinesis (PK), the ability to influence either objects or other people at will. The most famous practitioner of this is Uri Geller, who has become internationally renowned for his spoon-bending.

If psychic ability, or rather ESP (to use the correct term, made popular by American parapsychologist J. B. Rhine in the 1930s), can be proven to exist, its potential uses are widespread, not only for the gifted individual concerned, but for business, governments, and many other institutions.

The phenomenon of psychic detection is not a new one, although it hasn't yet received the same publicity as other areas of the "unexplained." Psychics have been solving life's mysteries for centuries, but the idea of them working with such institutions as police forces is surprising. Science fiction and the unexplained have become entangled in the public consciousness, especially in areas of psychic ability, so when we hear of a recurring phenomenon that doesn't fit into our current scientific understanding, we are all too quick to declare it to be fiction.

There are psychics who believe their intuitive powers can help them to help others, specifically in areas of crime and unsolved mysteries. For most of us, a hunch about a certain place or person is brushed aside as being irrational, but for

RIGHT: Harry Price, Britain's famous and flamboyant psychical researcher.

the psychic detective, being able to magnify and interpret such a hunch can potentially mean the difference between life or death.

The whole area is controversial, and as police forces are usually reluctant to admit they use the help of psychics, skeptics believe psychics tend to hijack the cases that have the potential to win them not only publicity, but financial reward as well. Yet, there are individuals who work with police forces time and time again, even those who are allegedly so successful that they only work on cases when they are invited to do so by the police.

Psychics have helped solve burglaries, find missing children, discover dead bodies, draw up photofits, locate untold missing objects, help construct psychological profiles, pick juries, and pinpoint the location of clues and weapons. Sometimes they even foresee a crime before it happens.

This book looks at specific cases and people who, it is alleged, have achieved the "impossible." They claim to have helped solve many crimes and mysteries. Can all of their stories and all the testimonies of the people they have helped, and even in some cases, the officers they have worked with, be put down to lucky coincidence? The existence of psychic investigators who work with police, should be an interesting starting point for ESP researchers.

It is not just the psychics themselves who deserve to be heard on the subject, despite the overwhelming evidence coming from

RIGHT: Dr. Sergeyev, Russian ESP researcher, demonstrates a bioenergy measuring device.

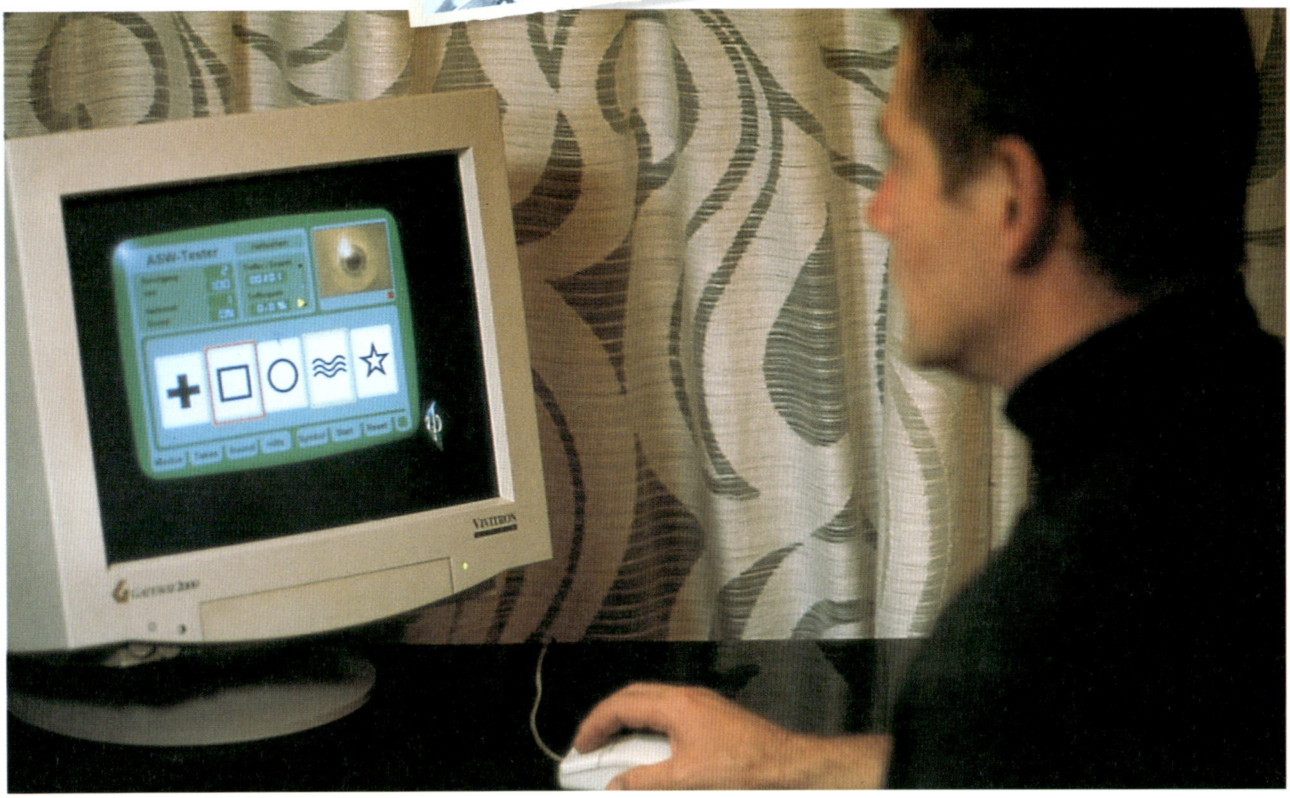

BELOW: A computerized ESP experiment where the sitter chooses random Zener cards.

those who believe in their powers. The skeptics, and there are many, put up more than one spirited argument against the existence of anything other than the reality we now understand. They argue that police forces waste time and money by listening to psychics, and that the police are far too easily taken in by "vague" clues that don't add anything to solving a case. Perhaps even more valid is the argument put forward that the psychics are trading on misery, that they are only causing even more emotional distress to families of victims by making wild assumptions and giving false hope.

While skeptics believe psychics are simply drawing on medieval superstition and are no better than witches, there are others who believe psychic powers definitely exist and that they are rooted firmly in the future. They believe psychics have somehow managed to tap into a resource that the rest of us have yet to understand and utilize.

This book tries to unravel this intriguing mystery, pitting skeptic against psychic and looking at some of the most exciting case histories. It investigates the history of psychic detection, from the early work of dowsers to the celebrated hunt for Jack the Ripper, the Victorian serial killer. It explores the idea that our ancestors were far more in tune with their own psychic sixth sense than we are today, and that this so-called gift that intuitives profess to have, may be part of us all.

Looking at the lives and cases of some of the most famous psychics who chose to channel their powers into helping the police, the book describes the extraordinary lives of people like the infamous Dutch psychic Peter Hurkos and the Illinois psychic housewife Greta Alexander. All these people have extraordinary tales to tell, their lives being dominated by the gruesome and painful reality of the world of crime. Many say they relive violent crimes, sometimes even "becoming" the victim and feeling the pain of an attack or murder. Some can allegedly foresee a crime before it happens, but have to live with the knowledge that there is very little they can do to change what is about to unfold.

The book explores the relationship between the regular crime prevention and detection forces, and those more unusual crusaders of truth, the psychic detectives. How, why, and when their powers work make fascinating and some-

ABOVE: Albert De Salvo is charged with the Boston Strangler killings. The police called in psychic assistance on the case, but followed their own hunches when it came to the arrest.

RIGHT: The red light district in Leeds, England, where the Yorkshire Ripper hunted his victims. The case triggered many "psychic" impressions of the killer, but few were of any use.

ABOVE: *New York cops read the latest on the Son of Sam killer. Had a psychic detective supplied the police with an accurate profile before the killer was apprehended?*

times contradictory reading. From dream interpretation, to "reading" the energy vibes from a murder weapon, methods as well as accuracy differ widely.

Psychic detectives are mostly individuals who come to their "profession" through word of mouth, but now ESP is also becoming big business. There are professionally organized groups who work specifically with the police, there are centers that specialize in "remote sensing" the whereabouts of lost children, and there are even psychic organizations that will use precognition to make a fortune on Wall Street!

As with any potential untapped source of power, there have been attempts to capture, manipulate, and use the power of ESP—and from institutions that you would not immediately associate with the paranormal. Certain police forces have conducted their own experiments to try to establish whether there is such a thing as ESP, but even more surprising is the secretive research carried out by large corporations and governments.

The development of government-trained psychic spies does seem, at face value, to be conspiracy-theory-style science fiction, but the proof is there. Both the Central Intelligence Agency and the former KGB have admitted involvement with psychic research, in particular the development of psychically gifted personnel whose powers can potentially be used to spy on an enemy. As with all such areas, the available facts are sketchy and scattered with false leads and misinformation, but the truth remains that some of the most compelling evidence for the verification of psychic detection comes from within government files.

By presenting first-hand accounts of how psychic detectives say their sixth sense gives them special knowledge, reports of a diverse array of cases, testimonies from police officers, results of official studies into ESP and detection, and the opinions of the skeptical community, we can gain an insight into whether psychic powers play a genuine role in police detection. On one hand, we could be on the very edge of discovering one of the biggest breakthroughs in scientific understanding ever, on the other, we could be sadly deluding ourselves that anything remotely unusual is happening. Are the psychic detectives extraordinarily gifted individuals who should be applauded for trying to make a difference in Western crime-ridden society? Whatever the truth—and it may be quite some time before science gets a grip on the ESP phenomenon—their story is intriguing and sensational, and will make you question your understanding of reality.

ABOVE: *Britain's renowned police headquarters are more wary about taking the advice of psychics, compared to their American colleagues.*

CHAPTER ONE

The Sixth Sense Investigators

Psychic Detection Through History

Most cultures have legends of talented seers who had visions predicting the onset of doom, or located missing objects or people. Many nomadic and tribal cultures have maintained a strong sense of this mysterious force, which helps make sense of everyday life. Today's Western version of the wise woman, the witch, or the medicine man, is more likely to work from an office, be connected to the Internet, and probably has a manager or public relations person to handle their affairs.

Psychic detectives have a long and increasingly troubled history. In ancient times, their words of wisdom or prophecies would have been taken at face value, with the same reverence a religious leader's instructions would have been adhered to. Now, as we believe ourselves to be highly sophisticated individuals operating in a world dominated by the rationality of the computer age, the majority of us dismiss the advice of a psychic as a harmless bit of fun.

How then do we explain the fact that certain police forces have admitted involving psychics in some of their most difficult cases? One Californian police department has even issued guidelines to its officers on how to get the best results from working with psychics. Skeptics would argue that not only are we in danger of wasting large amounts of public money, we run the risk of false convictions and needlessly inflicting more trauma on the victims of crime. Some scientists who are researching into this phenomenon believe we are on the edge of discovering a very real "sixth sense," which we will all be able to tap into.

Controversial as the topic is, there are some remarkable cases on record that seem to uphold the ability of certain individuals to use a power outside our current understanding to help get to the bottom of particular crimes. Throughout the world, police forces respond differently to advice from so-called psychics, yet, during the relatively recent history of the psychic detective, some of the most skeptical officers have found themselves telling reporters "I just don't know how she did it!"

The history of psychic detection includes some of the most infamous crimes of modern times … and the work of psychics trying to solve these cases is often just as fascinating as the mystery of the crimes themselves.

When Peter Sutcliffe began his campaign of terror in Leeds, England, in 1979, he triggered off one of the largest police investigations ever conducted in Britain. The press dubbed the man responsible for the frenzied attacks on women, "the Yorkshire Ripper," alluding to that other infamous murderer of prostitutes, the elusive Victorian Jack the Ripper.

By the time the police apprehended Sutcliffe, almost six years after his first brutal attack on twenty-eight-year-old mother of four, Wilma McCann, he had viciously murdered and mutilated thirteen women. Seven more were deemed extremely lucky to be alive. The public was in uproar as the investigation dragged on, and the police were at their wits' end with very few clues. The one source of information that did seem to be forthcoming, however, was from the psychic community.

Scores of letters relaying dreams, visions, hunches, and even sketches of the guilty individual arrived on the desks of the West Yorkshire Constabulary. Many more were sent to the tabloid newspapers, whose obsession with the salacious details of the murders and the victims' backgrounds meant they needed a steady flow of new angles on the story.

The Sunday People newspaper commissioned Doris Stokes, the U.K.'s most famous clairvoyant, to use her psychic powers to determine what the Ripper looked like. The paper then devoted pages to the resulting sketch an artist constructed with Stokes' help and also published her other psychically divined "feelings" about the murderer.

The Daily Star, a rival paper, went one better and published "psychic" drawings of friends and family of the Ripper, as well as giving various psychics' impressions of names, dates, places, and people connected

BOTTOM: Newspapers led the way in generating thousands of responses from the public in the hunt for the Yorkshire Ripper, including psychic clues to the killer's identity.

BELOW: Peter Sutcliffe, pictured in the cab of his truck, was eventually caught thanks to conventional police work rather than through psychic detection.

Dream Detection

Numerous books claim to be dream dictionaries, analyzing the symbolism of our strange imaginings that take place in a twilight world of slumber. Dreaming of running a race for example, is often interpreted as a sign that you are striving hard to achieve something, but other symbols are not so clear. Dreaming of a cat is considered unlucky, yet to dream of seeing a pile of manure is a good-luck sign!

Most ancient cultures have placed great significance on dreams as omens, and in most major religions dreams have played an important part in conveying God's message to his chosen subjects. In more modern times, psychoanalysts, such as Freud and Jung, have also believed dreams are an important state where our subconscious mind shares information with our conscious mind.

Divination (the art of seeing into the past or future) via the study of dreams, has a long tradition. It is well known ancient Egyptian pharaohs employed interpreters to foretell their futures. However, few psychic detectives rely on dream states to solve crimes. One notable exception to this is the British psychic Chris Robinson (see pages 72–3; 76–7), whose dreams have proved so accurate in predicting crimes that he has been dubbed the "dream detective," and he has helped police all over Britain. Robinson's dreams started in 1989 and took a great deal of interpretation. He doesn't dream events exactly as they happen, but has gradually become able to recognize various symbols. For example, in his book, cowritten with journalist Andy Boot, Robinson discusses how he realized the significance of dogs in his dreams—they represented killers, or the IRA.

Even places are symbolic in Robinson's dreams, so he writes down everything. Because Robinson works through his dreams, trying to make sense of what his subconscious is trying to convey, there have been times when he has made mistakes. In one case, Simon Jones, a four-year-old toddler, had vanished from a park in Hertfordshire, England. Robinson tried to "dream" what had happened to the child, despite being in the middle of deciphering other dream-information about terrorist attacks. His dreams seemed to be telling him the boy was dead, he had been buried, and his abduction was connected to a fairground. The boy was, thankfully, found alive some weeks later.

ABOVE: Nella Jones, one of Britain's most famous intuitives, has claimed she gained accurate facts about Sutcliffe from her unusual talents.

with the crimes. None of them were any help to the police and even Stokes' predictions, according to skeptic James Randi, that the perpetrator was called Johnny or Ronnie, were way off the mark.

There was one psychic, however, Nella Jones, who claimed to have given the police details which, she says, if they had been heeded, could have captured Peter Sutcliffe eighteen months before he was finally arrested. The British psychic says she sent a sketch, the name Peter, and even the murderer's address to the police. Considering the West Yorkshire Constabulary received thousands of such reports, they can perhaps be forgiven for ignoring this one that claimed to be right. If someone had paid attention to the amateurish sketch and Jones' predictions gained by going into a trance and visualizing the killer, would twenty-year-old student Jacqueline Hill and forty-year-old office worker Margueritte Walls still be alive today?

Fortune-tellers of the famous

The work of psychics helping to solve crimes is still a controversial area. Strangely, the publicity these paranormal practitioners receive is generally positive. Their work only makes the headlines when a sensational case, proving impossible to solve, is suddenly kick-started again by the sixth sense of a modern "witch."

Police spokespeople have gone on record declaring they were amazed by the information a certain psychic gave them, various "intuitives" have actually lectured to U.S. police departments, and the American government has allegedly carried out research, compiling case histories, to examine whether psychics are actually useful in aiding criminal investigations.

On January 18, 1999, *The Guardian*, a British newspaper, reported how Moussa el-Moghrabi, an eighteen-year-old Palestinian man, was imparting clairvoyant advice to various members of the Palestinian cabinet. His fame was spreading in the region and he had already been dubbed the "Palestinian Rasputin." While the paper wasn't suggesting President Arafat had his personal coffee dregs "read" by the hairdresser-turned-psychic, it did report that "about half of Mr. Arafat's cabinet are said to carry Moussa's charms in their pockets."

LEFT: Moussa el-Moghrabi, the "Palestinian Rasputin," whose psychic predictions are not only advising leading politicians, but are also making news internationally.

BELOW: Even the U.S. president, Bill Clinton, is believed to have sought psychic advice on how to handle the public aftermath when the Lewinsky scandal broke.

That wasn't the first time powerful world leaders have reportedly put their faith in what some people would consider nonsense. When Cherie Blair, the wife of British Prime Minister Tony Blair, was pictured wearing a "new-age" necklace, the press was in uproar. Other stories, such as former First Lady Nancy Reagan's alleged preoccupation with charting her husband's horoscope daily and President Clinton's supposed hiring of the "intuitive" Salvador Lunes Collazo to advise on the consequences of his affair with Monica Lewinsky, have baffled some and pleased others. If important world figures believe there is something more to our psyche than is at first obvious, perhaps the rest of us are missing something.

Psychics who can be classified as working "psychic detectives" have a long history. Over the years, murderers have been caught; missing people and bodies located; incriminating evidence brought to light; rapists, sadists, and thieves apprehended; stolen property found; kidnap victims rescued; treasures, oil, and gemstones successfully mined for; and enemies successfully spied on and thwarted. There have also been a lot more unsuccessful predictions. Is it a simple case, like the skeptics suggest, that when almost 2,000 psychics contact police, then the chances are at least one of them will be near the facts?

There are cases, though, where inexplicably, a premonition about future events has proved to be uncannily accurate, and where the details of such have been recorded for all to see. In the novel *Black Abductor*, published in 1972, author Harrison James wrote about a white, wealthy female student who was kidnapped by an extremist group who gradually brainwashed her into accepting their ideas. Two years later, the infamous kidnapping of Randolph Hearst's student daughter bore so many similarities to the novel that its author was at first considered a suspect. Both actual and fictitious girls were called Patricia, both terrorist groups had a black leader, both girls ended up joining the kidnappers, both had boyfriends with them

ABOVE: Patty Hearst's 1974 kidnapping bore so many similarities to an earlier novel, that its author was considered a suspect. Coincidence or psychic ability?

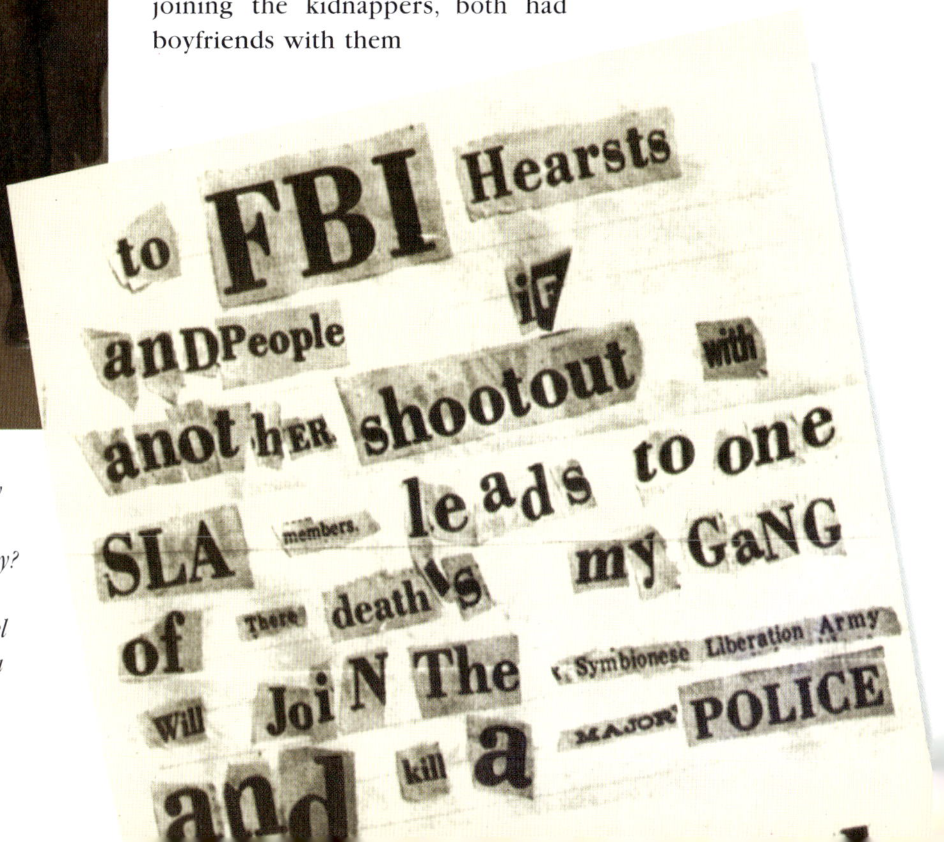

RIGHT: The kidnappers in both real life and the novel were members of a violent extremist group led by a charismatic black leader.

The Victorian Psychic Sleuth

The story of Robert James Lees has become confused and facts have been blurred by fiction with the passing of time. This is mainly because the records of his involvement were written by Lees himself, many years after the events he described took place. Lees purported to have solved one of the most infamous criminal investigations ever. He said he led the police to Jack the Ripper's front door.

Jack the Ripper was responsible for five murders over a space of three months in 1888. Some researchers have speculated there were other victims, and indeed as no-one was ever tried for the crimes, many people at the time believed the Ripper continued to be responsible for a variety of murders and assaults. The identity of the Ripper is still not known, although there has been vast speculation, with suspects ranging from lunatics, doctors, royalty, and even a woman—"Jill" the Ripper.

The victims were all from the East End of London, and all were prostitutes. Whoever it was who mutilated and then murdered the women was obviously knowledgeable in the art of surgery, because all the victims bore wounds indicative of a skilled, and ruthless, butcher.

ABOVE: The Jack the Ripper case was—and still is—notorious for its horrific brutality perpetrated against prostitutes.

ABOVE: Robert James Lees, who became more famous for his visions of Jack the Ripper than for his writings.

A royal psychic advisor?

Robert James Lees was a known clairvoyant and had even given demonstrations of his talents to Queen Victoria, the first of which was when he was only nineteen. Some sources say Lees was the Queen's psychic advisor, but it is doubtful his influence was that great. It has been documented, though, that Lees worked as a journalist and also wrote books on his experiences with the spirit realm. He tended to have visions that gave a clue of events to come, and he was certainly famous for his time.

According to Lees's own account of his involvement with the Ripper case, he had a vision preceding the second murder, in which he saw the

"Lees's third and final vision was apparently even more vivid than his first. He went to the police who, from his own accounts, were so impressed by his descriptions they took him straight to the most recent crime scene."

whole sickening event played out in front of him. He saw a woman and a man walking together down a narrow lane. The woman appeared to be drunk and a clock showed him that the time was about 12:30 at night. All of a sudden the woman was dragged into a doorway, her throat was cut and when her body gave way, she was horribly mutilated. The attacker wiped blood from himself and wrapped a long coat or cloak around his body before disappearing into the night.

The vision so disturbed the psychic, he went straight to Scotland Yard Police Station, but as no similar murder had been reported, he was treated with disdain and told to go home. Some versions of the story say he was immediately questioned as a suspect in the case—a pitfall that many psychics have attested to experiencing. The night after Lees's vision, the Ripper struck again, in much the same manner as the psychic had described.

The second vision wasn't as clear for Lees, but he did see a woman's ears being cut off. Despite the previous ridicule, he was convinced he had somehow tapped into the Ripper's world, and he once again went to the police. This time they were more interested because a letter had been sent to the Central News Agency and passed to the police, supposedly signed "Jack the Ripper," threatening that he would "clip the lady's ears off and send to the police officers just for jolly wouldn't you."

Murders and mutilations

Sure enough on October 1, Catherine Eddowes's body was found with a portion of her earlobe missing. Her body and the body of Elizabeth Stride were the results of a double Ripper attack that the perpetrator had told police to expect in the same letter where he threatened to remove an ear. The butchered earlobe was never sent to the police. A postcard, received by the Central News Agency on the same day that the bodies were discovered, and written in similar handwriting to the first note, said Jack hadn't had the time to get the ear to the police.

Lees's third and final vision was apparently even more vivid than his first. He went to the police who, from his own accounts, were so impressed by his descriptions they took him straight to the most recent crime scene. From there, Lees allegedly led the police through the streets of London telling them that he knew who they were looking for. He led them straight to the front door of a respected doctor, Sir William Gull. The doctor's wife told police that her husband sometimes acted very strangely and been missing for periods that would seem to have coincided with the various murders. Although he was mostly a gentle man, he sometimes had violent fits of rage and could be cruel, she added.

Whether Lees had taken police officials to the right house is still debated. Certainly, Gull was detained in a private asylum, but he was never declared guilty. Although the murders are thought to have ceased at this point (even that is debated by Ripperologists), the police carried on with their investigations.

ABOVE: Sir William Gull was never charged with the Ripper murders, despite Lees's certainty of the doctor's guilt.

at the time of the kidnap, and both girls' fathers were conservative and wealthy. Had the kidnappers read the book, or as they say, is fact stranger than fiction?

Foretelling the fate of the Titanic

One such case of precognition, or the ability to see into the future, could be explained away as coincidence, but an equally chilling testimony to its powers was published more than 100 years ago in 1898. A book, titled *The Wreck of the Titan*, told a gripping tale of a grand ocean cruiser that hit an iceberg and sank on its maiden voyage. When the news of the terrible tragedy of the sinking of the luxury ship called the *Titanic* shocked the world in April 1912, it wasn't long before parallels were drawn between the disaster and the fictitious sinking. The specifications of the ships were remarkably similar, let alone the other obvious comparisons. Was it simply fluke that author Morgan Robertson conjured up a plot that later manifested itself in reality, or was someone trying to relay a warning about the tragedy to occur in fourteen years' time?

"Psychic detective" is really a modern term for a group of people who believe their extrasensory skills give them an insight into a side of life or another realm most of us close our minds to. For centuries, people have tried to answer life's problems by approaching a "gifted" few. Even today when the West is so obsessed with wealth, fame, and striving for happiness, the most rational of people consult their horoscopes daily to help them navigate through their lives.

BELOW: The Titanic *sets out on her maiden voyage from Southampton, never to return, just like her fictitious counterpart, the* Titan, *fourteen years' earlier.*

If—and as yet it hasn't been conclusively proved whether there is or there isn't—there is an intuitive sense that can be tapped into, to either foresee the future or unravel the past, then the implications for our lives are incredible. Not only on a personal level, but on political and military levels as well, harnessing the power of the mind could provide the first person to do so with the key to untold wealth and power. Perhaps it has already done so.

Is it this wealth and power that motivates certain people to claim they have these incredible talents? Certainly, the world's most famous psychics have

The Dead Detectives

Doris Stokes was probably the most well-known medium of recent times. She was famous for her motherly approach and her seemingly uncanny ability to contact spirits from the "other side." The spirits not only had everyday messages for their loved ones, but sometimes gave Stokes an insight into crimes that had or were going to happen.

Contacting the spirit world has a long tradition that goes back farther than the birth of Spiritualism as a movement in the West, in 1848. Shamans, priests or priestesses with magical powers, have consulted spirits from other worlds in an attempt to answer the questions of their people since recorded history began. They were, in essence, the first spiritual leaders man had, and their importance in the development of all cultures illustrates the essential need man has to make sense of his place on earth.

Shamans work in many ways to help seek advice from beyond our earthly realm. Traditional tribal shamans—such as those from Native American, Aborigine, or African indigenous populations—often conduct rituals where they leave their bodies to travel on the astral plane to seek advice from the inhabitants of the netherworld. Others are mediums, who let their bodies or minds be taken over by the spirit world. In effect, they allow themselves to become possessed. Although this practice can take on what we in the West consider alarming characteristics, epitomized by traditional voodoo mediums, psychic detectives, such as Stokes, use mediumistic talents in their work which are not dissimilar to these ancient traditions.

Those who were fortunate enough to witness Stokes at one of her many performances, were often amazed at how easily she appeared to be able to clear her mind and slip into a light trance. Her body was never taken over by spirits, as some mediums claim, but she said she heard their voices in her head very clearly and then passed on the messages to the relevant people. She conveyed the messages, more often than not they were mundane and only interesting to the person they were intended for, in her own voice. She always maintained there is life after death and the spirit world is capable of keeping an eye on our material one.

gained a notoriety from their alleged powers that would have otherwise been denied them. Daniel Dunglas Home, the most respected British psychic of his time, mixed with the likes of the poets Elizabeth Barrett Browning and her husband Robert, the Empress Eugénie of France, Count Tolstoy, and eventually married a goddaughter of Czar Nicholas of Russia. Today's so-called psychics don't quite make royalty, but they do advise them occasionally. Not long before Diana, Princess of Wales died, for example, she famously visited psychic Rita Rogers.

Uri Geller, the well known Israeli intuitive, claims to have made at least part of his fortune from using his paranormal powers to locate oil and precious mineral deposits for large companies. Without doubt Mr. Geller has amassed his wealth and notoriety from his alleged extraordinary powers. Before he became well known in this field, he was an advertising model and worked the nightclub circuit. Now he is internationally famous, has mixed in circles that have included

BELOW: Daniel Dunglas Home gained an exclusive following through extraordinary demonstrations of clairvoyance and levitation at his séances in both America and Europe.

Psychometry: Good and Bad Vibrations

Psychometry is probably the most common method used by those working as psychic detectives, to help focus their thoughts on how, where, or even why a crime was committed. The method is based on the idea that we all emit an aura of energy that is absorbed by any object we come in contact with. So, for example, a trained psychometrist is able to hold a person's wedding ring and tell them accurate information about themselves.

The nature of psychometry means it is generally only useful for helping unravel the past, but the objects used to divine information from vary widely: Single stones or bricks can allegedly store information about buildings; clothes can record information about their owners; and even photographs are supposed to somehow capture some of a person's aura. (Certain hill tribes in Southeast Asia, for example, believe the camera is evil because they think it captures a person's soul when it takes a picture.)

While most police departments are very unlikely to part with crucial evidence, such as a murder weapon, so a psychic can divine the details of the crime for them, victims' families have often provided psychics with clothes, photographs, or other personal items, which they hope the psychic will be able to use to glean information.

Dorothy Allison, the New Jersey psychic detective who often works with local police forces, specializes in locating missing children. Like many psychics, she says when there is great emotional distress, as there obviously is when a child disappears, the ability to home in psychically is stronger. Allison uses psychometry to focus her thoughts on a particular child. She asks for a photograph of the child, and from that, picks up on the energy of the particular individual, especially whether he or she is still alive. From the starting point of the photograph, her psychic skills are then focused onto what has happened to the child. Describing the information as coming through to her as on a TV screen, Allison also, somewhat disturbingly, has said that she ocasionally witnesses the crime from the perpetrator's point of view.

ABOVE: Uri Geller poses with his cutlery-covered Cadillac of "psychically" bent spoons and forks. Geller has made his fortune through his unexplained powers.

John Lennon and Salvador Dali, and claims he has been asked to work on covert operations by the CIA.

In a sense, most work carried out by intuitives can be described as detective work. They are consulted for answers to questions the majority of us cannot solve; for instance, whether our loved ones are with us although they have died, what our future might hold, or if we want to find a missing object. Psychic detectives, however, specialize in using their powers to enter the world of criminal investigation.

What do we mean by ESP?

The term ESP (extrasensory perception) encompasses a wide area of as yet unexplained "talents," which haven't generally been well received by the scientific community. While the popular conception of psychics and mediums—the difference between the two will be explained shortly—is of someone not far from being a witch, in fact, ESP is more common than most of us think.

ESP, the ability to glean information about someone, something, or somewhere, using an ability which as yet hasn't been identified by science, covers three broad areas. Firstly, there is telepathy, which is the apparent

ABOVE: Clairvoyants use crystal balls to focus their minds on a specific question, rather than "seeing" events in the ball, as is commonly believed.

Did the Dead Solve the Mystery?

Although the fashion for mediumship has waned since the late 1800s and early 1900s, there are still psychic detectives who believe their talent, or at least their insight, is directed by contact with the dead. Most of us are aware of the black-and-white photographs of mediums producing ectoplasm from various orifices and strange forms being materialized in the dark by notorious Victorian mediums. We also now know many of the "stage" physical mediums were talented tricksters, often with very willing helpers.

The psychic detectives who work with police, yet still believe they are directed by the dead, don't tend to employ such theatrical manifestations these days. Chris Robinson, Britain's "dream detective" (see pages 72–3; 76–7) has come to the conclusion his dreams are directed by the spirit world, because this explanation makes the most sense to him.

ABOVE: The ghostly wreckage of airship R101. Intense flames destroyed most of the ship.

The mysterious flying machine

One particular case of psychic detective work seems to back up the theory that the special insight some intuitives receive is actually passed on from "the other side." On October 4, 1930, the British R101 airship, whose glamorous destination was India, took off with its VIP passengers, heading toward France. In the early hours of the following morning, disaster struck the huge silver airship. What happened exactly will never be known, but somehow the ship was flying too low and exploded. Only six people survived and forty-eight perished. All that was left of the airship, when daylight came, was an eerie skeleton. Neither the remains or the survivors could shed much light on what had gone wrong.

A week after the crash a séance was being held in London. The aim was to contact the spirit of the author Sir Arthur Conan Doyle, who had died that same year. The medium in attendance, Eileen Garrett, was one of the best known at the time. Garrett was quite extraordinary: She never attempted to explain her talent and subjected herself to rigorous tests in front of some of the harshest critics. Her ability to contact spirits from the "other side" was aided, she said, by her spirit guide Uvani.

The attempt to contact Conan Doyle was arranged by one of Britain's ardent skeptics, Harry Price, a paranormal investigator. Price had arranged for a skeptical journalist and a shorthand secretary to record impartially what happened during the séance.

LEFT: Eileen Garrett. Did her mediumship help spirits of the dead crewmen solve the mystery crash?

"Incredibly, Vickers was able to hold a conversation with his dead colleague through Garrett. It seemed Irwin's spirit was desperately trying to make sure the truth was known about the disaster."

Garrett, after going into a trance, suddenly got extremely upset and her voice changed to that of a man's. To everyone's surprise, the voice of the R101's captain, Flight-Lieutenant H. Carmichael Irwin shakily addressed the room. *The Unexplained* magazine later reported that "the voice kept rising and falling, hysteria barely controlled, and the speed of delivery that of a machine gun. Price and Coster [the journalist] were amazed as a torrent of technical jargon began to tumble from the lips of Eileen Garrett."

Did Captain Irwin return?

Through Garrett, the distraught spirit of Irwin seemed to be explaining the mystery of what had happened to cause the airship disaster: The engines were too heavy; the fuel composition wasn't right; the altitude needed couldn't be reached; trials hadn't been comprehensive enough—the list of faults and mistakes seemed to go on and on.

This was not the only time Irwin's spirit tried to solve the mystery of the tragedy. Again with Garrett acting as the medium, Irwin spoke to his friend Major Oliver Vickers. Incredibly Vickers was able to hold a conversation with his dead colleague through Garrett. It seemed Irwin's spirit was desperately trying to make sure the truth was known about the disaster. There was much speculation in the newspapers at the time that the official inquiry into the R101's explosion would involve a cover-up, so the government department responsible would not be held to account.

While the official inquiry refused to take the medium's message seriously, Vickers was not the only intelligent person convinced that Irwin's testimony from the other side was actually what happened. It seems highly unlikely Garrett (who was never proved to be anything but genuine) could have hoaxed so many eminent people with her technical knowledge of the airship's design. Whether Irwin's spirit actually came back from the dead to solve the mystery, however, is still the subject of great debate.

ABOVE: *Squadron Leader E. L. Johnston, Major G. H. Scott, and Captain H. C. Irwin, pictured before the fatal flight.*

The Guardian Angels

One of most extraordinary cases of otherworldly crime prevention is discussed in the book Life After Death and the World Beyond, by paranormal authors Jenny Randles and Peter Hough. A British woman, only identified as "the wife of a well-known television presenter," experienced problems with her car, so she pulled off the highway to wait for assistance. When another car stopped, she lowered her window and was terrified when the driver grabbed her ignition key and forced his way into the car. He pointed a gun at her and instructed that she remove her clothes.

At this point, Randles and Hough report, an intense bright light filled the car and appeared to be the shape of a man. "She felt an instant rapport with this being, but it was too much for the would-be attacker, who got out, ran back to his own car, and drove off at speed." The light disappeared when the woman was no longer in danger. She believes a guardian angel saved her from the attack.

Does the above case indicate that at times when the channel of a medium simply isn't practical, a spirit being can directly interact with our world to prevent crimes or disasters?

ABOVE: Palm reading at the Palisades Amusement Park, New Jersey. Crime-solving psychics rely less on such traditional methods, instead preferring to tune in to their psi powers.

ability of two or more people to connect their thought patterns, even at a considerable distance. Secondly, there is clairvoyance, which is the detection of facts about a person, place, or object using this unknown gift. Thirdly, there is the ability to "see" into the future, called precognition. All these elements come into psychic detective work, and however the individual psychic makes sense of his or her powers, we can at least try and make sense of their claims using the references of ESP.

When those funny little coincidences happen, such as telephoning a friend just as they were going to call you, or saying the exact same thing as a family member for no reason, or answering a question before a partner has actually asked it, or the special relationship twins supposedly have with each other—these can be put down to ESP. All these events happen to the majority of us and we pass them off as being everyday things, but they aren't that far removed from having vivid dreams that seem to have some meaning for the future, or getting a "feeling" about a particular place you have never been to before. Or, perhaps even seeing what you think is a ghost.

All ESP is, however, is the experiencing of feelings or having reactions that are outside the realms of our ordinary five senses. Most psychics say anyone can learn to use these talents, because it is just a case of tuning into this "sixth sense." In the last century psychics were more often known as "sensitives," which accurately describes how they saw themselves as naturally being more open to whatever it is that causes ESP. Greta Alexander, a well-known American psychic who worked with police many times from the 1960s to the 1990s, said her sixth sense was like "watching television inside my head. I become the antenna and I just pick up the picture."

How and why certain people seem to be more tuned into things that the majority of us can not comprehend, hasn't yet been verified. From the old gypsy idea of being the seventh child of a seventh child, to more modern theories of left-brain states and electromagnetic energy, the key to the riddle of psychic energy—if there is one at all—could lead us to a whole new understanding of how we function.

Understanding the psychic mind

While the study of such an exciting subject is revolutionary and controversial, some caution should be applied. What is true beyond any doubt, is that there are large parts of our brains we have yet to understand. We are only at the beginning of understanding mental illness, and we are even farther behind understanding the link between our conscious and subconscious, so any investigation into the area of ESP must be conducted carefully, especially if the enthusiast is to convince skeptics.

Equally so, the phenomenon known as "psychic detection" should not be taken as a proven ability. Indeed, until the majority of police forces publicly verify they work with psychics, we cannot be positively certain of their usefulness in aiding the fight against crime. On the other side of the coin, however, there are undoubtedly extremely generous and intuitive individuals who may well be a positive source of information for the police. Everyone involved has their own agenda: Distraught parents will often try any avenue, no matter how small the chances of it helping, to find a missing child; psychics have a vested interest in providing "vague" clues, which can easily fit any or every type of a particular crime; and the police are just as likely to cover-up the fact they have resorted to asking a psychic for help, for fear of looking incompetent

and because of the general public's nonacceptance of psychic powers.

As well as all the problems associated with using well-meaning psychics, there are the unfortunate cases of deliberate fraud. In 1981, for example, Tamara Rand, a Beverly Hills psychic who tended the rich and famous, suddenly became the most talked about psychic in America—but for the wrong reason.

A tape of a television appearance by Rand on a Las Vegas talk show, apparently recorded on January 6, 1981, showed her predicting the then president,

BELOW: In order to "feel" with their sixth sense, psychics often need to shut out the information being relayed by their other five senses, to enable them to focus properly.

Divine Magic

Tuning into energy using the skill of dowsing is still used, and can allegedly be big business. Water companies and even oil companies employ "twitchers" to walk over promising sites with their dowsing rods, trying to pick up energy that is transmitted. This has a scientific reasoning behind it, because running water and oil both emit a detectable electromagnetic field, which a dowser's pendulum or twitching sticks can pick up. Mining companies looking for metals and gems have also employed diviners. The Geller Effect, an autobiography of Uri Geller, coauthored with Guy Lyon Playfair, contains photographs of Geller working with mining companies in the Solomon Islands and Brazil, using dowsing to help the companies find gold.

It is not only objects that a dowser can find. Some dowsers allege they can tune into emotions as well, and just as Frenchman Jacques Aymar managed to lead police on the complex trail of three fleeing murderers (see page 32), other psychic detectives have used dowsing to help solve crimes. In the seminal work on dowsing, The Divining Hand by Christopher Bird, the author tells the story of Vo Sum, a Vietnamese Naval Captain. Vo Sum's father had been interested in dowsing and had shared his beliefs with his son, but the younger man had not really used the technique until he was older and suddenly regained his interest in it as a method for finding lost or missing people and things.

From photographs, Vo Sum was able to divine whether people were alive or dead, and according to Bird's book, realized, by trying to find the whereabouts of the living, he had discovered the geographical locations of North Vietnamese prisoner-of-war camps. Vo Sum also helped the South Vietnamese navy plot the course of missing ships. He was particularly successful in tracking down the position and course of a smuggling vessel in 1974, which was carrying 2.1 tons of raw opium. Vo Sum's dowsing not only gave the coordinates of where the ship would be found, but at what time, on what day, and what drug the smugglers were carrying.

ABOVE: The 1981 assassination attempt on President Reagan. Tamara Rand claimed she foresaw the event, but was later accused of concocting a hoax.

Ronald Reagan, was going to experience a "crisis time" in late March or early April. She went on to say she thought it might be an assassination, there would be gunshots, and a young, fair-haired, radical man would be involved. She even gave the name as something like "Jack Humbley." Sure enough, an assassination attempt on the president was made on March 30, 1981, and police arrested a twenty-five-year-old, blonde-haired man called John Hinckley. The videotape of Rand making her predictions was supposedly rediscovered and ended up being broadcast on all national U.S. TV networks.

Yet, according to Gary P. Posner, writing in the book *Psychic Sleuths: ESP and Sensational Cases*, "skeptical Associated Press reporter Paul Simon discovered the tape had actually been produced the day after Reagan was shot, with the complicity of Rand's friend, Las Vegas columnist and TV personality Dick Maurice." Maurice eventually confessed to helping the psychic with a hoax. However, Rand remains adamant there had been a mix-up with the tapes.

Not all supposed psychic successes have been submitted to such minute dissection and very often we are left with only the psychic's side of the story. The more the predictions of people calling themselves psychics are recorded, and the more they allow themselves to be monitored and tested, as in the case of Eileen Garrett (see pages 28–9), the easier it will be for investigators to attempt to explain whether psychic detection really does harness an unknown sixth sense, or whether it is simply a waste of time and public money.

Following a bloody trail

One of the earliest recorded cases of psychic detection was in 1692, in France. In what is an excellently documented (and almost certainly genuine) case, Jacques Aymar solved the murders of a Lyons wine merchant and his wife, with the help of his divining rod. The police were understandably skeptical about Aymar's twitching rods, and tested him further when he pronounced the murders had been committed by three men.

The rod, though, was faithful to its master and seemingly twitched when it was on the right trail of the men. Aymar and his escort simply followed its movements through the countryside and to the gate of the prison in the town of Beaucaire, where he told police one of the men was already situated. Sure enough, a man being held on a different charge of theft, eventually admitted he had been party to the murders when he was faced with Aymar and his divining rod. He gave the names of the other men involved to police and was eventually sentenced to death. The police were so impressed, and the story got such widespread publicity, that Aymar was asked to help on other investigations.

In the seventeenth-century case above, dowsing was the particular method used to focus the sixth sense, but other techniques have also been applied with supposedly accurate results. While

LEFT: A seventeenth-century French dowser with his twitching rod positioned correctly.

ABOVE: Kate (left) and Margaretta Fox became the first public mediums after their initial encounter with a spirit.

LEFT: The girls often gave séances, revealing their powers, but later in life were accused of fraud.

methods such as dowsing may have their basis in scientific fact, skeptics find other methods more of a problem to comprehend. This is especially true with those psychic detectives who believe their insight is provided by a direct link with what is often called "the other side."

Doris Stokes was an old-style psychic, relying on her clairvoyance to reveal clues and messages. She didn't primarily work as a psychic detective; generally she gave sittings and worked as a traditional medium, relaying messages from the dead to their living relatives. Her work reflected a long tradition dating back to the Fox sisters, American girls who made contact with a spirit in 1848, who tapped out its responses on the walls of their parents' home in Hydesville, New York. Their spirit guide allegedly helped them locate the body of a man who had been murdered and buried in the basement.

The Fox sisters have sometimes been credited with being the first psychic detectives. The spirit came though to the girls, telling them he had been a traveling salesman and he had been violently robbed then killed by "C. R." The spirit also said his body had been buried in the cellar of the house. Neighbors and friends all gathered to witness the strange tappings and conversations between the Fox family and the spirit, and someone soon remembered a previous occupant of the house had been called Charles Rosana. When the basement was finally examined, parts of a skeleton were found. Rosana was traced, but only with the evidence of a so-called spirit, there was little anyone could do to bring him to trial.

It is perhaps this uncomfortable relationship, which today is a common misconception, between psychics and the dead or the "otherworld," which leads such down-to-earth agencies as the police to dismiss psychic predictions as "rubbish." But few psychics working in the field of detection today make claims about working with spirits. Their methods usually vary slightly, but most would agree their gift is nothing supernatural, it is simply a part of their consciousness, which the majority of us have either suppressed or refused to acknowledge.

ABOVE: Psychic detectives often work with a photograph of the missing person or murder victim, believing it can store important information in the form of energy.

Anyone can do it!

Certain psychics, such as American Dorothy Allison, who works with New York and New Jersey police and specializes in finding missing people, claims anyone can be taught to be more psychically tuned in to the world around them. Kathlyn Rhea, a Californian psychic who also specializes in finding bodies, likewise believes psychic powers can be developed with practice and training. She believes all of us have the talent to tune in to whatever the sixth sense is and all we need is someone to teach us how to develop it. When Marcello Truzzi interviewed Rhea, she told him she not only works finding missing people, but also helps with jury selections and advises legal teams. "I tell them how a certain judge is going to react in a case, what points they should stress, and what they should gloss over." Is this the future for professional psychics?

Most working psychic detectives, and there are increasing numbers who not only work in conjunction with police departments but have set up private agencies, use psychometry, dowsing, remote viewing, and visualization to "receive" their clues. Crimes that involve a major trauma, such as murder, abduction, rape, and runaways, seem to be the easiest for the psychic to hone in on. Psychic detectives generally find it difficult to explain how their sixth sense works, but say they somehow manage to shut off outside influences while they hold an object belonging to the victim, or maybe even a murder weapon. The emotion linked to the object allegedly triggers a flow of information, in the same way that poring over a map of an area or simply concentrating on a person's profile can also do.

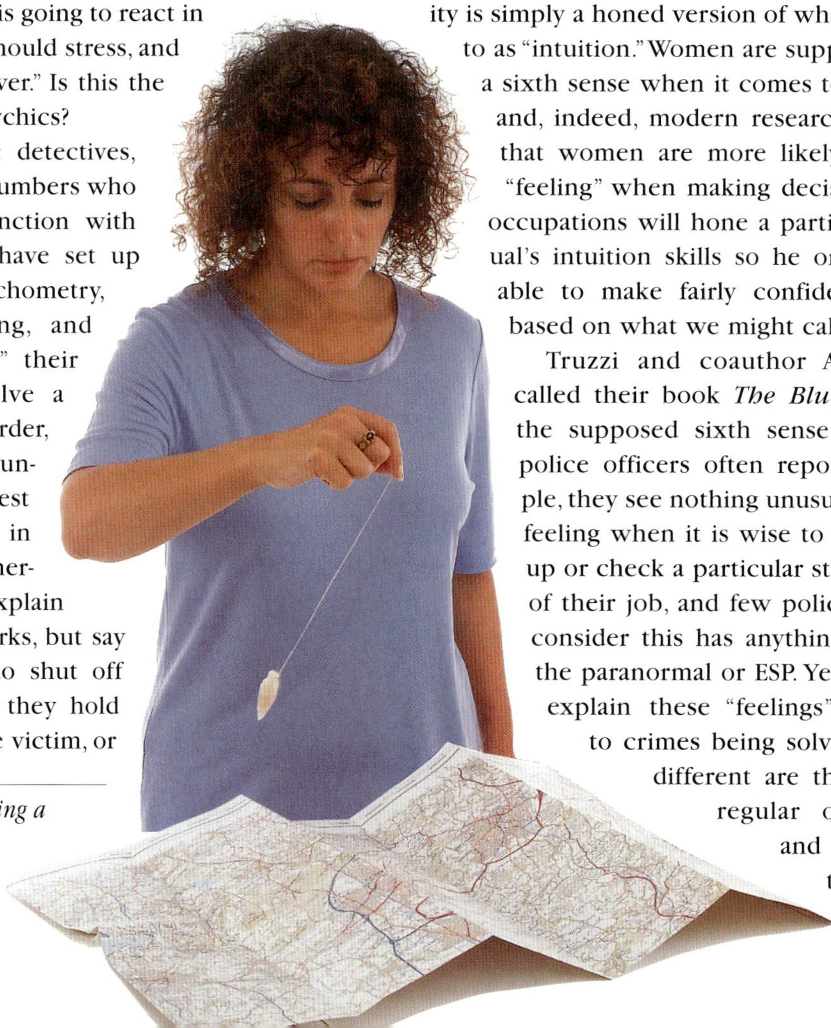

RIGHT: Dowsing over a map using a pendulum can help to home in on a particular area.

Some researchers speculate that the psychics' ability is simply a honed version of what we all refer to as "intuition." Women are supposed to have a sixth sense when it comes to daily living, and, indeed, modern research has shown that women are more likely to use this "feeling" when making decisions. Certain occupations will hone a particular individual's intuition skills so he or she will be able to make fairly confident decisions based on what we might call a "hunch."

Truzzi and coauthor Arthur Lyons called their book *The Blue Sense* after the supposed sixth sense that regular police officers often report. For example, they see nothing unusual in having a feeling when it is wise to call for backup or check a particular street. It is part of their job, and few policemen would consider this has anything to do with the paranormal or ESP. Yet, how do we explain these "feelings" which lead to crimes being solved? And how different are the hunches a regular officer feels, and the information a psychic

Turning On and Tuning In

Some psychic detectives do not seem to need an object or method to help concentrate their psychic perceptions. Instead, they say their impressions just come to them—like visions suddenly appearing in their heads or seeing an act played out in front of them. Often the easiest way for the psychic to explain this, is by comparing the vision to a TV screen or movie.

Nella Jones, a British psychic who has been connected in the media with many large cases, including the hunt for the Yorkshire Ripper, became a psychic detective out of the blue. Although she has always claimed to have known she was psychic, coming from a family with a long tradition of the sixth sense, her entry into the world of crime fighting was sudden.

Jones was watching a TV news broadcast in February 1974, which reported how a valuable painting by the Dutch artist Jan Vermeer, called "The Guitar Player," had been stolen from the Kenwood House museum, in London. As she was watching the news report, she claims she went into a light trance and "saw" in her head where the painting had been hidden. She sketched a map of the area and pinpointed the painting with a cross and led the investigating officers to where the alarm system used to protect the painting had been discarded and partially hidden. Some sources say the frame of the painting was found at the same point.

Jones also told police that the painting would be discovered in a cemetery, in good condition, but not until after a ransom note was delivered by the thieves. She seemed to believe the graveyard was the well-known Highgate Cemetery in London, but the painting was not found there. It was, in fact, eventually discovered six miles away in another cemetery. Jones maintains it had been moved there via Highgate.

Marcello Truzzi and Arthur Lyons, in their book The Blue Sense, reported that Jones's psychic visions, which came from out of nowhere and played in her head like a movie, impressed the police. Police Detective David Morgan, from the Hampstead Police, credited Jones with "leading the investigation forward."

detective receives? The debate gets even more complicated. There are police officers who also claim to be psychics or mediums—although there are very few who publicly admit this—and they say their sixth sense helps their work considerably.

The NYPD Blue Sense

Riley G. is an ex-New York police officer who now works as a psychic detective, allegedly helping his colleagues track serial killers, find lost children, and locate hidden bodies. It is unusual for the two worlds to cross over, but Riley G. says he used his ability throughout his time as a law enforcement officer. He claims he saved not only his own life, but also that of his partner, on more than one occasion by foreseeing events that were just about to happen.

He is typical of most modern psychic detectives when he tries to sum up his extraordinary "gift." "For me it comes in flashes in my mind. I see the events as they happened, or are happening. I can sense what the killer or suspect sees at the time of the crime. I also pick up certain visions from holding murder weapons and I can use a form of remote viewing. I do actually have to switch off my abilities. I deal with the most cruel and abnormal side of human nature, and I have to take time out for my own sanity. I feel that we all as individuals have a fair amount of psychic ability, but we must learn to bring them out of ourselves."

BELOW: Riley G., ex-NYPD cop turned psychic detective, claims his intuitive visions have saved his own life.

CHAPTER TWO

The Psychic Profile

A Who's Who of Psi Detectives

Despite the controversial nature of their work, some psychics have established considerable reputations around their alleged ability to help solve mysteries and crimes. Most shun publicity and work quietly, keeping low profiles, but some, like the psychic detectives discussed in this chapter, have become the "stars" of their chosen field.

Much of the information about particular psychics comes from their own files and memories, so it is crucial to remember the incredible success stories claimed by individuals often represent one-sided points of view. Many of the psychics profiled here, however, have worked time and again with police departments or other agencies who have consequently publicly endorsed the individual psychic's abilities.

The life stories of the psi detectives are fascinating. Most have come from humble beginnings and almost always refused to accept payment for their talents. Their generosity, almost across the board, and willingness to travel, spend their own time and money, and the incredible strain of dealing with emotionally challenging situations, can only be applauded. Although skeptics have been quick to pick holes in the information provided by psychics, and the methods by which this information is obtained, being a psychic detective is not an easy job.

Despite all the criticisms, these individuals have been approached by the authorities when all other hope of solving a crime has vanished. Are they testimony to the fact we should be paying attention to the powers of the "sixth sense"? Are there genuine cases when a psychic has solved a murder, a kidnapping, or a robbery?

Gerard Croiset, one of several famous Dutch psychic sleuths, was declared genuine by one of his country's leading parapsychology professors after their meeting in 1945. In Bulgaria, a state-run hotel had to be built near the humble home of the blind psychic Vanga Dimitrova because so many people wanted to visit the wise woman. Greta Alexander, the American psychic detective who died in 1998, specialized in finding lost children. She employed a team of secretaries, had two offices, and numerous phone lines to deal with the volume of requests for help she received. Each of these fascinating stories will be told in this chapter.

PETER HURKOS: THE DUTCH DETECTIVE

A profile of Dutch psychic Peter Hurkos, published in *Out of this World* (Volume Four), says, "He sees through sealed envelopes and brick walls. He has only to look at a man or woman to know their darkest secrets. It is enough for him to pass his fingertips over the back of a photograph to know whether its subject is living or dead." Hurkos was certainly one of the most famous psychic detectives of modern times, yet his career as an out-of-the-ordinary psychic sleuth contains many not-so-glowing accounts of his activities.

When he died of heart failure, aged seventy-seven, on June 1, 1988, his obituaries credited him with being the extraordinary psychic who helped police on such infamous cases as the Boston Strangler and the Manson family murders. He was also linked to many smaller crimes, mainly missing persons or murder cases, both in his home country of Holland and around the world.

Most of the information about his work comes from the psychic himself, and even his obituaries were "briefed" by his Hollywood publicist. The records of many cases were compiled by him and mostly documented in his autobiography *Psychic: The Story of Peter Hurkos*, which critics accused of being overly enthusiastic about how accurate he was. Yet, he modestly admitted, "I have never claimed more than 87.5 percent accuracy in my readings."

LEFT: Peter Hurkos became famous world-wide for his psychic crime-solving abilities and regularly made the headlines in national newspapers, as well as appearing on TV shows.

BELOW: Hurkos allegedly came up with the name "Charlie" after visiting the scene where Sharon Tate and her friends were murdered by the "family" of Charles Manson.

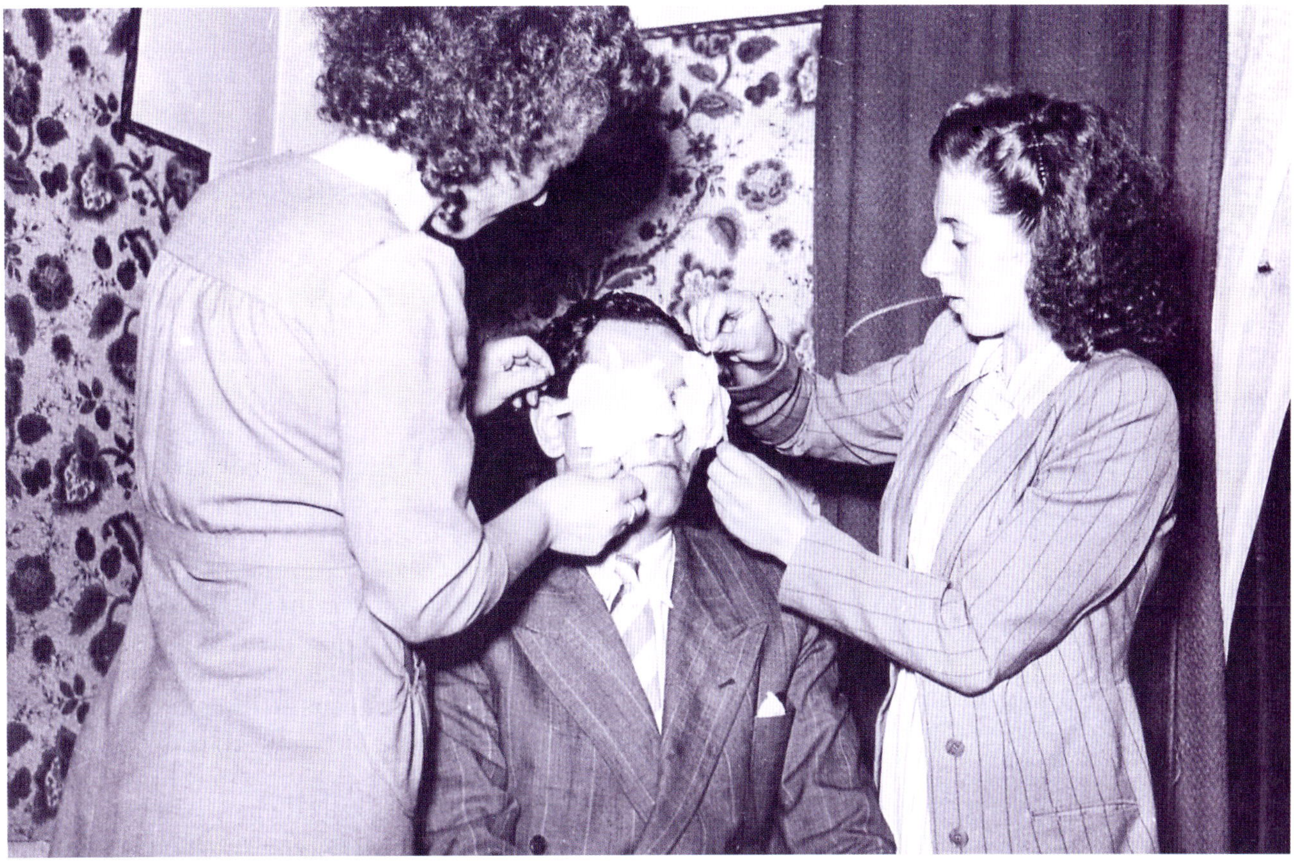

Hurkos's younger years

ABOVE: The Dutch detective underwent many tests throughout his career as a psychic, but skeptics have always managed to find fault with the various methods used. Here he is having his vision blacked out, in preparation for an experiment.

Originally called Pieter Van der Hurk, Hurkos was born in Dordrecht, Holland, on May 21, 1911. He didn't think he was psychic in any way when he was young, although his mother apparently read cards for people, predicting their futures. She, in fact, told her young son he would leave Holland eventually and end up living somewhere where English was the main language. Sure enough, Hurkos moved to America in his later life.

The family was not well off and Hurkos had to leave school at sixteen to work in his father's house-painting business, and there were three other children to feed and clothe. He also worked as a sailor, as well as helping his father in the summers, and when World War II broke out and Holland was occupied by the Germans, Hurkos worked for the underground movement, allegedly helping sabotage German military operations. He changed his name to protect his family in case he was discovered, and thereafter was always known as Peter Hurkos.

An accident triggered the young Dutchman's psychic powers, when he fell thirty-six feet from a ladder while helping his father paint a house. He landed on his head and shoulders, and was lucky to live. Hurkos spent three days in a coma, and after he regained consciousness had to be hospitalized for a considerable time. It was then he began to experience strange sensations, while he lay in his hospital bed. He seemed to be able to understand what people around him were thinking, or be able to "see into" a part of their lives. It upset him at first, and he said the doctors were completely puzzled by his sensations.

A 1953 article by Theodore J. Beck, published in *Fate* magazine, documents how when Hurkos warned a nurse of a trivial event which he thought might happen to her soon, she was astonished, because what he described had taken place the week before. The same article describes how "on one occasion, the thoughts of a nearby patient interfered with his own rest to such a degree that he burst out, 'It's your own fault. Your father hasn't been dead for three months and you have already sold the clock he prized so much. Why did you do it?'." His neighbor was dumbfounded.

Trying to save a secret agent

Hurkos's own recollections of his hospital stay included the dramatic prediction that a fellow patient was actually a British spy. He just sensed that the man, who was about to be released, was going to be killed on a nearby street called the Kalverstraat by the Nazi occupiers. He tried to warn the man, but no-one took his claims seriously—a problem he seems to have encountered throughout his psychic career—and according to Hurkos, the events unfolded a few days later, just as he had predicted.

How true the above account is, however, is questionable, because some dedicated researchers have tried to trace the records of the mysterious British agent, but none apparently exist. It does seem odd that there are no local town records of a murder taking place, yet, maybe the whole event was covered-up by the Nazis themselves.

Acknowledging that he did possess an extraordinary gift led Hurkos to become well known locally for being able to "read" the past, present, and future of people around him. Hurkos described himself as a psychometrist: "I can touch things and then tell you what I see—information about them just comes to me." In his autobiography he described his strange powers as "I see pictures in my mind, like a television screen." And he told an interviewer in *Psychic* magazine, published in the March/April 1970 edition, that when he touched an object or person and then let his mind go blank the impressions he got were like "a movie. And I have to forget about my private life, my family life. I have to blank everything out. Then I get this feeling, and somehow make mental pictures, like a TV picture." He claimed to be able to divine everything about a person, just by shaking his or her hand.

Hurkos arrived in Britain in 1950, during the uproar after the Scottish Stone of Scone was stolen from Westminster Abbey in London. The Stone has a long history of being the seat upon which ancient Scottish kings were crowned, and it had been kept in the Abbey since it had been brought to England by Edward I in 1286.

The psychic claimed that Scotland Yard had asked for his assistance, but unsurprisingly, the renowned police force denied this. Hurkos was, however, granted access to various bits of evidence, but his predictions weren't followed up. He left England annoyed and described the British police as "cold and unbelieving." The police eventually found the Stone without his help, but Hurkos claimed he knew where it was all along, and that he had predicted it had been stolen by students as a prank, which it was.

Despite Hurkos's disillusionment with the British police, he became extremely well known throughout Europe. It didn't seem to matter how accurate he was; if his name was linked with a crime and the crime was

LEFT: The ancient Stone of Scone, back in its rightful place under the Coronation Chair. Hurkos claimed he was asked by the British police to help locate the missing stone.

Hurkos and the Strangler Case

The involvement of Peter Hurkos with the Boston Strangler case has also been a murky area, especially as the man eventually arrested was not the man Hurkos picked as the killer. Yet, there is little doubt he was invited by the police to help with the case.

Between June 1962 and January 1964, the people of Boston, Massachusetts, lived in a state of fear as a sadistic, perverted killer roamed the streets preying on women of all ages. He was nicknamed the Boston Strangler, because after sexually assaulting his victims, he would garrotte them, usually with an item of the victim's clothing. He often mutilated the women with cuts and bite marks.

Thirteen women, aged from nineteen to eighty-five, died in this manner, and the police were desperate to track down the perpetrator. Hurkos was allegedly called in secretly—for the police to admit they had asked for the help of a psychic was like telling the killer they had no idea who he was.

Hurkos was given access to an extraordinary amount of primary evidence, which he worked with for six days. He was allowed to handle clothes, underwear, and bedsheets from the victims, which according to one source, he slept with to help him focus. When he was given a letter written to the nursing director of the Boston School of Nursing, requesting that she find its author a wife from her nurses, Hurkos knew he had found the killer.

The letter reinforced mental images he had been getting about the killer, some of which came to him while in a fitful sleep. He had shared these with police and it didn't take long to track down Thomas O'Brien (a pseudonym). He was fifty-seven years old and fitted the physical build and background as described by Hurkos.

DID THE STRANGLER GET AWAY?

A month later, Albert De Salvo, a man being held on a rape charge, confessed to being the Strangler. He gave a long account of his crimes, yet there were certain areas that he appeared to have no idea about. He was tried on previous charges, because there wasn't enough evidence to convict him for the murders, but the case of the Boston Strangler was closed. De Salvo was sent to prison for life, and later murdered in his cell. Hurkos always claimed the police had got the wrong man.

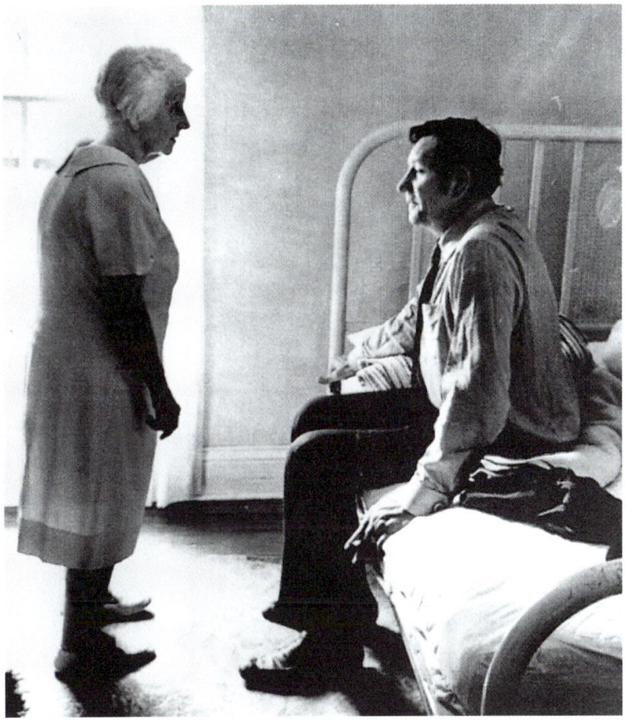

ABOVE: Hurkos, pictured in 1969, examines a suspect's room in the case of the Coed Killings. He allegedly touched all the walls and furniture, and kept repeating the word "Canada."

then solved, the public believed in the man who had become psychic after falling from a ladder. Investigations by skeptics have uncovered a host of embellishments and exaggerations on behalf of the psychic, yet his reputation as one of the most successful psychic detectives of the century lives on.

DOROTHY ALLISON: FINDING THE LITTLE ANGELS

Dorothy Allison, an American housewife and full-time psychic detective, is one of the most famous psychics working with the police today. She specializes in the location of missing children, and according to her most ardent fans, some of whom are working police officers, she has a good track record in finding them.

Allison realized she had a gift for locating missing people when, in 1967, she had a vision that involved a dead little boy who was wedged inside a pipe under water. She went to the Nutley, New Jersey, police (Allison lives in Nutley) and told them her story. Subsequently, local papers reported the body of Michael Kurcsics, aged five, was found in exactly the same manner as Allison had described from her vision.

ABOVE: Dorothy Allison stands on the tranquil riverbank in Clifton, pointing to the spot where Michael Kurcsics was found after his body had been swept down river.

RIGHT: Arguably the most well-known psychic detective in the U.S., Allison not only receives much media interest, but has to fend off the attentions of skeptics keen to discredit her.

Salvatore Lubertazzi, a police detective in Nutley who regularly worked with Allison, has said he didn't believe in psychics until then. Interviewed in a July 1979 edition of the *Law Enforcement Journal*, he said, "It's a very strange feeling to go up to this woman and tell her what I'm looking for and she describes the area and it's miles and miles away … she's found twenty missing or deceased persons for us since 1968."

Although Allison has claimed her mother was psychic, and that she has had visions all her life, it wasn't until the incident with the dead five-year-old boy that she says she realized she could put her talent to valuable use. Since then, her visions have come thick and fast, and she allegedly has bags full of letters from desperate parents and police

ABOVE: David Berkowitz received a 365-year sentence for the Son of Sam killings. He was also believed to have had links to a Satanic group.

RIGHT: Stacey Moskowitz, the killer's last victim, is taken to hospital where she later died as a result of the July 31, 1977, shooting.

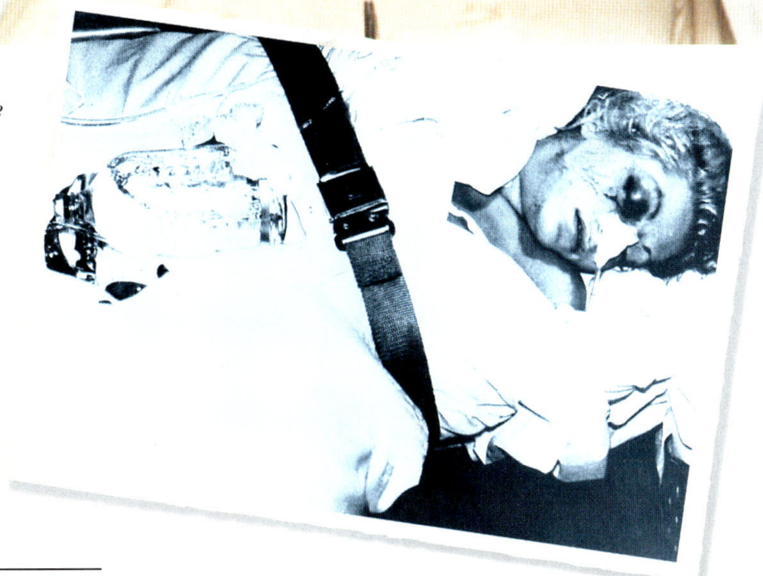

departments alike. She claims to have successfully worked on such high-profile cases as the Son of Sam killings and the Patty Hearst kidnapping.

Working from home

Never charging for her work with missing children, Allison simply asks that her modest expenses be met … and, if possible, she asks for an "affidavit" from the police department she has worked for. This is not always forthcoming because of the prevailing stigma of using psychics on official investigations, but individual officers have been keen to praise the work of the Nutley housewife.

Being down to earth is evidently part of Allison's appeal. She has said in interviews that she is repelled by the crimes she witnesses third hand and that she would like to "smack their faces," referring to the perpetrators. She adds she "won't stop as long as little children get murdered." She keeps a scrapbook of pictures of all the children she has helped locate, whether they were found dead or alive, and refers to them in interviews as "little angels."

Reader's Digest magazine ran a feature on Allison in December 1978 headlined "The Woman Who Sees Through Psychic Eyes." In the article, Allison was pictured with the numerous police badges she has been given by the departments she claims to have helped with investigations.

One of the cases highlighted by the *Reader's Digest* was that of missing fourteen-year-old Susan Jacobson from Staten Island, New York. The girl's parents were convinced police were wrong about the missing girl when the investigating officers decided it was a classic case of a runaway teenager, her parents insisting this was out of character. At the end of May 1976, three weeks after their daughter had disappeared, the Jacobsons contacted the psychic. Allison and her husband went straight to the Jacobson house and accurately told the distraught parents Susan's birthday and time of birth. After demonstrating that she had "picked-up" on Susan's presence, Allison went on to say she knew Susan was dead and described images of things she saw in the general area of where her body would be found. The Jacobsons located a place which could only have been the one Allison had described, but it covered such a wide area they asked the police to help search it. Understandably, perhaps, the police were reluctant because the information had been provided by a psychic, and they had already carried out extensive searches.

Almost two years after her disappearance, however, Susan's body was found by three boys—in the area that had been predicted by Allison. The discovery of

The Atlanta Killings

Dorothy Allison received mixed publicity when she traveled to Atlanta in October 1980, with a view to helping solve a particularly nasty serial killer case. At least once a month for more than a year, a child was taken from the poorer area of Atlanta. Police were at their wits' end. When Allison was asked to get involved with the case, the police had recovered ten bodies and four were still missing. Although she vowed to the press and public that she would remain in the city until the killer was found, she actually left within a week of her arrival, saying she had given the police all the information she could.

Allison maintains she was successful. She says she gave the name of the murderer to the police along with valuable clues about his background and whereabouts, but the police, in retrospect, were not so sure. Some newspapers quoted Allison directly, saying she had provided the police with just two names, one of which was correct. Other reports quoted police working on the case who said she did, indeed, give them names, but there was a whole list of them to work through. In subsequent interviews, the police claimed that Allison's information was so varied and wide-ranging it was impossible to follow up. However, Allison is adamant she has a tape-recording in which she can be heard giving the correct name of the killer to the police.

BELOW: Just two of the newspaper reports detailing Allison's involvement with Susan Jacobson's mysterious disappearance.

Identify Girl's Skeleton

The skeleton of a girl found Thursday on Staten Island was identified yesterday through dental records as that of ...n Jacobson, 14, of 30 Anderson Av... Richmond, S.I., who had be... May 1976. ... said the ...

N.J. psychic joins hunt for girl missing on Island

By JANICE KABEL

The Jacobson family's search for their missing 14-year-old daughter Susan has taken on a new dimension in the world of the sixth sense.

Two weeks ago, the Port Richmond famil...

...caro of the Nutley police force, "Dorothy is reliable." He has worked with her on solving several cases in New Jersey and the pair traveled to California and "worked with the FBI" on th...

...which no one outside the family could know. "That's what convinced me," Mrs. Jacobson says.

That same day...

the remains led to the arrest of a youth by the police; he was eventually charged with Susan's murder. The Jacobsons were finally able to bury their daughter.

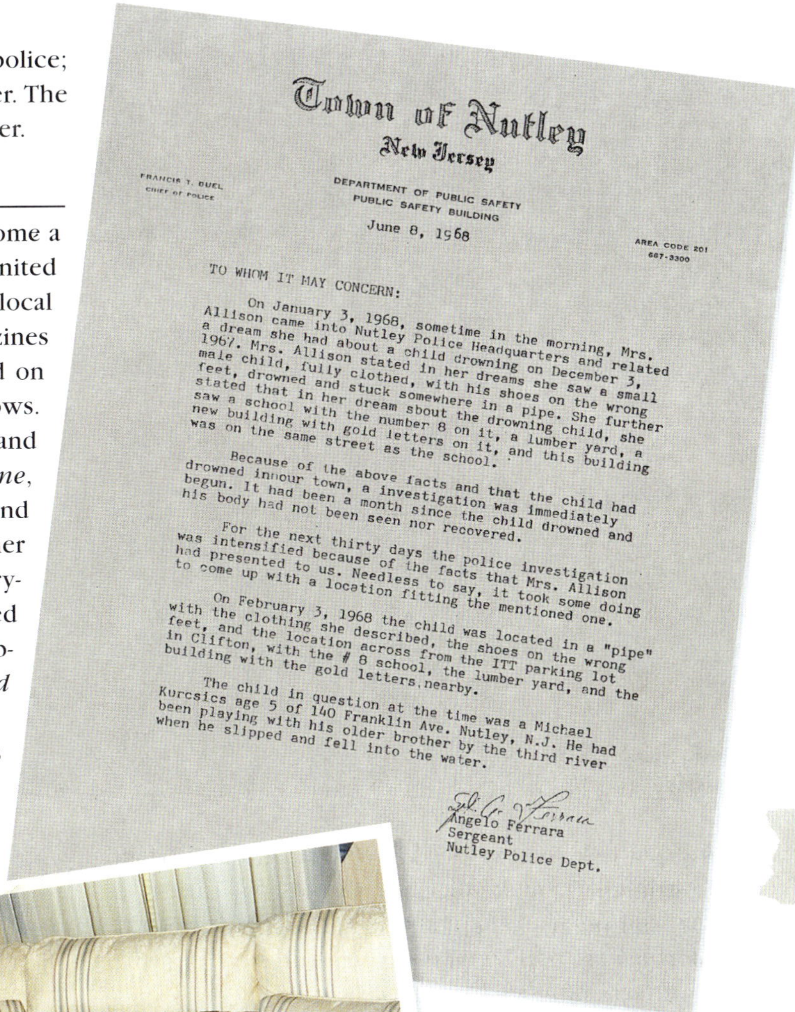

Town of Nutley
New Jersey

FRANCIS T. BUEL
CHIEF OF POLICE

DEPARTMENT OF PUBLIC SAFETY
PUBLIC SAFETY BUILDING

June 8, 1968

AREA CODE 201
667-3300

TO WHOM IT MAY CONCERN:

On January 3, 1968, sometime in the morning, Mrs. Allison came into Nutley Police Headquarters and related a dream she had about a child drowning on December 3, 1967. Mrs. Allison stated in her dreams she saw a small male child, fully clothed, with his shoes on the wrong feet, drowned and stuck somewhere in a pipe. She further stated that in her dream sbout the drowning child, she saw a school with the number 8 on it, a lumber yard, a new building with gold letters on it, and this building was on the same street as the school.

Because of the above facts and that the child had drowned innour town, a investigation was immediately begun. It had been a month since the child drowned and his body had not been seen nor recovered.

For the next thirty days the police investigation was intensified because of the facts that Mrs. Allison had presented to us. Needless to say, it took some doing to come up with a location fitting the mentioned one.

On February 3, 1968 the child was located in a "pipe" with the clothing she described, the shoes on the wrong feet, and the location across from the ITT parking lot in Clifton, with the # 8 school, the lumber yard, and the building with the gold letters.nearby.

The child in question at the time was a Michael Kurcsics age 5 of 140 Franklin Ave. Nutley, N.J. He had been playing with his older brother by the third river when he slipped and fell into the water.

Angelo Ferrara
Sergeant
Nutley Police Dept.

Not all publicity is good publicity

Allison says she shuns publicity, yet she has become a psychic star, probably *the* psychic star of the United States. She has been the subject of numerous local newspaper stories, has featured in major magazines such as *Time* and *Newsweek*, and has appeared on the *Oprah Winfrey* and *David Letterman* TV shows. Despite all the media hype about her abilities, and her seeming humility (she told *Police Magazine*, "Money's not my God. My gift came from God, and I would never sell it. I wouldn't use it for other purposes either, so long as there are mothers crying"), Allison features among a distinguished group of psychic detectives who come in for substantial criticism in *Psychic Sleuths: ESP and Sensational Cases*, edited by Joe Nickell.

In an article entitled "America's Most Famous Psychic Sleuth," investigative writer Michael R. Dennett questions whether all of Allison's claims can be taken at face value. Dennett asks some pertinent questions, particularly about what happens when Allison, although she is only one example out of many, gets it wrong. What if, he asks, the wrong person is sent to jail on the words of a psychic?

Dennett says he asked Allison for examples of the hundreds of letters she supposedly received from police departments verifying she successfully helped on investigations; he was sent only three. Delving into some of Allison's more recent cases, Dennett hypothesizes that some of the clues she gives to police are so vague they have the potential to be fitted into a scenario which then gives the impression of accuracy. Here we have the perennial problem. Like many psychic detectives, Allison has never claimed 100 percent accuracy and maintains she simply passes on her psychic impressions, while skeptics demand infallible proof. If she says a range of numbers is significant and only one in the range

ABOVE: *Allison has amassed a huge number of police hats, badges and certificates from various departments she has worked with over the years. This impressive collection is a testament to how busy she has been, working on police cases.*

turns out to be part of an address or an assailant's date of birth, for example, then the skeptics raise an eyebrow and point to the numbers she has got "wrong." Unfortunately, psychic impressions are just that, not a list of facts produced by the clairvoyant. Allison gets extremely angry at this sort of public denouncement, although to her credit, she receives a lot less general criticism than most psychic sleuths. She maintains she never offers help to the police unless she is asked. Besides which, she says she has worked on more than four thousand cases, and believes there are very few where she hasn't managed to help in some way. One of the highest profile and most controversial cases Allison has assisted with is that of the Atlanta murders.

A genuine desire to help

Despite some negative publicity, even Dennett admits Allison is not out to make money and she genuinely believes in helping people. Indeed, Allison comes in for considerably less criticism than many others featured in *Psychic Sleuths*. She is even credited with personally paying for little Michael Kurcsics's funeral because his parents weren't able to.

Allison not only has visions, she also uses psychometry, most often with photographs of the missing children, to help her concentrate on clues. She says she

ABOVE: Dorothy Allison, flanked by (left to right) Detectives Henry Antovino, Don Vicaro, Anthony Intile, and Edward Guerino, of the Nutley Police Department.

works some eighteen hours every day, and that, although she has the potential to make quite a bit of money from her fame, she has only truly profited from sales of her autobiography. In an interview with reporter Mary Jo Patterson in *Police Magazine*, Allison recounted how she "floats clues" within her visions which, when properly interpreted, can solve "even the most puzzling crimes." This "interpretation" of Allison's clues is the key to her success. The information she gains psychically is not black and white and, more importantly, it does not seem to be time-specific. So, while she could have a vision of a particular location, that place may have been somewhere the child had been even before he or she disappeared—or it could be that the vision is of the place where the body will be found.

Admitting she has no sense of direction, her "interpreter" police detective Lubertazzi knows when Allison says "north," it might be better to head south. Similarly if she sees numbers, they may not always occur in the order they appear in her vision. After years of working with the psychic, Lubertazzi seems to have become adept at unscrambling Allison's psychic information. It is quite a recommendation that Lubertazzi's superiors allow him to work with the psychic in police time—they obviously believe the housewife from Nutley has a gift worth nurturing.

GERARD CROISET: THE PSYCHIC WIZARD

Gerard Croiset was yet another world-famous psychic detective who was born in Holland. Like Peter Hurkos, Croiset's career was peppered with sensational cases and equally sensational predictions with a high accuracy rate, but again, like Hurkos, Croiset faced some harsh criticism. What distinguishes Croiset from other psychic detectives, is the sheer volume of cases that he is said to have worked on, and also his unique association with a professor of parapsychology, who not only recorded Croiset's cases, but backed his claims to the hilt.

Croiset had a disturbed and unhappy childhood. He was born in 1909 to unmarried parents; his father was far from attentive either to him or his mother, and his mother gave him and his brother up for fostering when he was only eight. According to Colin Wilson's book *The Psychic Detectives: Paranormal Crime Detection, Telepathy and Psychic Archaeology*, Croiset first revealed he had psychic abilities at the tender age of six. This is very unusual among those who have claimed to be psychic detectives, because most of them have had some kind of trauma which sparks off their gift. Yet, intuitives who describe themselves as clairvoyants, as Croiset later did, often say they have had the gift since birth.

Wilson's book describes how the young Croiset told his teacher he knew why the schoolmaster had not been there the day before, saying the young man had "been to see a blonde girl who wore a red rose." The teacher had, in fact, been to see his girlfriend to propose marriage. Although this small example is perhaps incidental, it was the start of a much more glamorous career. Initially, as a young adult, Croiset worked at various menial jobs, only using his psychic talents to amuse friends and help people he knew. Allegedly his reputation in the town of Enschede, where he was living with his new wife, grew and many more people started coming to him for help. Needing a wage to live on and realizing there was a demand for his special gift, Croiset opened a psychic healing center, which was to become not only popular, but also profitable.

LEFT: Gerard Croiset first demonstrated his psychic powers at school, when he was only six.

A fantastic reputation

The Blue Sense, Truzzi and Lyons' book, pays considerable tribute to the Dutch psychic. It recalls how he was alternatively known as "The Wizard of Utrecht," "The Man With the X-Ray Mind," and even the "Mozart or Beethoven among Clairvoyants." The two writers document how it "is claimed that he solved many of the century's most puzzling crimes, found scores of lost objects, and hundreds of missing persons. He is said to have performed hundreds of paranormal healings, and occasionally demonstrated extraordinary powers of precognition by correctly foretelling future events."

The Psychic Detectives: Day One

IS THIS WH

RIPPER

The town where a killer could be

DEREK SHUFF

ABOVE: Croiset's impressions of the Yorkshire Ripper hit the headlines.

LEFT: Critic Dr. Jule Eisenbud was not impressed by the results of Croiset's chair tests.

This seeming "superstar" of psychic circles may never have become famous outside his hometown of Enschede if it hadn't been for one particular evening. Apart from his unorthodox method of supporting his wife and son by using his healing "magnetic hand," his life could have taken a much quieter path if he had not attended a lecture in December 1945 when he was thirty-six years old. The lecture was given by Dr. Wilhelm H. C. Tenhaeff, who was a doctor of parapsychology at the University of Utrecht. After the talk, Croiset approached the older man and told him about his powers. Tenhaeff had already published a number of books on the subject, and had worked with other Dutch psychics, testing their claims. It appears he was intrigued by the young man in front of him, and he resolved to carry out some tests on Croiset.

The meeting sparked a long friendship and mutually beneficial working relationship between the two men, which would take them all over the world on the trail of murderers, missing children, and stolen objects. Tenhaeff later proclaimed Croiset to be one of the most remarkable psychics he had ever met, making Croiset the first psychic detective to receive a scientific validation by a university professor. Or so it seems—for subsequent investigations have cast doubts on their professional relationship.

Meeting his mentor

When Tenhaeff gave his lecture in Enschede, according to Truzzi and Lyons, he wasn't being paid by the university and funded his research through his published books. "In large part," the authors assert "as a result of the widespread publicity he and Croiset attracted, in 1951 the fifty-seven-year-old parapsychologist was officially appointed a teacher at the university and in 1953 he was given a full professorship." Many researchers have quoted journalist Norma Lee Browning's discovery that Tenhaeff's salary as a professor was paid by the Dutch Society of Spiritual Healers—an organization headed by Gerard Croiset!

Many of Tenhaeff's tests involved what he called "chair experiments," where Croiset would be shown an empty lecture theater or hall full of seats, where he would later be demonstrating. He focused in on several seats and made predictions about the people who would later occupy them. These tests were conducted long before tickets had been sold, so even the people who would eventually be sitting in the seats had no idea where they would be placed. Tenhaeff's records say Croiset was enormously successful at this trick, although it is of course less glamorous than his alleged success with crime solving.

American journalist Jack Harrison Pollack wrote Croiset's biography with the help of Tenhaeff, and he listed over seventy troublesome cases the Dutch psychic "wizard" supposedly solved for various international police forces. Wilson's book documents when Croiset helped the New York Police Department (NYPD) in the case of a missing four-year-old girl, Edith Kiecorius, over the telephone. Holding only a

ABOVE: The chair tests involved Croiset predicting details about individual members of an audience, who would be occupying certain seats at a later performance.

BELOW: The streets of New York City, where Croiset helped locate a missing four-year-old child, despite being thousands of miles away in Holland at the time.

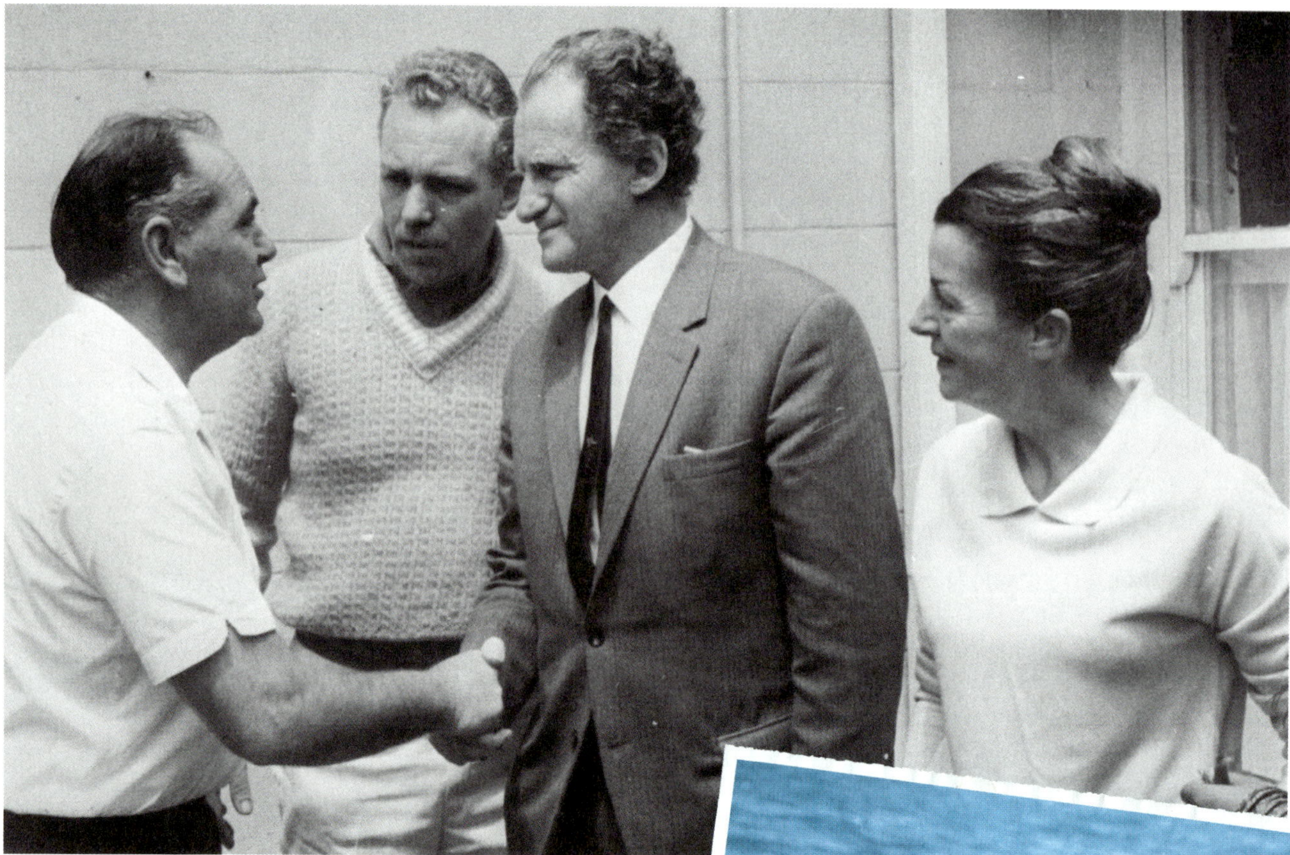

ABOVE: Croiset greets Jim Beaumont, whose three children disappeared from a beach in Adelaide, Australia. Local businessmen paid for the psychic to fly out to assist police.

photograph of the little girl and a map of New York City, Croiset was able to tell the NYPD the girl was dead. He described her killer and allegedly was accurate in describing where she had last been seen. The police were at that point following leads which suggested the girl had been abducted and was still alive. The investigation was changed as a result of Croiset's information, and Edith's body was found in a small, rented apartment. The room led the police to the killer, Fred Thompson, a man whom Wilson says fitted Croiset's description.

Another long-distance case, again in the United States, was a private investigation searching for a Professor Walter E. Sandelius's twenty-four-year-old daughter, Carol. She had disappeared from a hospital in Kansas where she was a patient. The professor had heard about the Dutch detective, and contacted Tenhaeff with the information about his daughter. Croiset telephoned the distraught father and gave a

ABOVE: An interpreter follows Croiset along the sea wall, recording the clairvoyant's impressions as he retraces the children's steps.

Solving a Scottish Murder

Gerard Croiset became famous internationally primarily because the police in his home country were far more open about their willingness to consult psychics. One of the cases which is frequently cited as extremely successful was the baffling disappearance of a young woman in Scotland.

Seventeen-year-old Pat McAdam and her friend Hazel Campbell were hitchhiking home the day after a party in Glasgow, on February 19, 1967. They were offered a ride by Thomas Young, a truck driver. Young went out of his way to drop the two girls off close to their homes. Hazel got out in Annan, saying goodbye to her friend and the driver. According to the story Young told police, he then dropped Pat off and went on his way. Pat was never seen again.

It took the police three weeks to track down Young, but he insisted he had let the young woman out near her home and had not seen her after that. Three years later the police were no nearer to finding out what had happened to Pat, until a Scottish journalist who had worked on the case traveled to Holland and asked Croiset for his help. He had a police poster with a picture of the girl and a map of the area, both of which he gave to the psychic. He had also taken the girl's Bible with him.

Croiset immediately told the journalist that Pat was dead, that she had been killed near a bridge, and her body dumped in the river running under the bridge. All this sounded very general—until Croiset described the area near the bridge. He said there would be a house with an advertisement board on one side, and a car with no wheels against which leaned a wheelbarrow. Croiset claimed Pat's body would be found lodged in the roots of trees in the river.

The bridge in Croiset's description was located and, uncannily, there was indeed a house, car, and wheelbarrow close by, just as he had predicted. Pat's body was never found, however, and it is believed it had washed away.

The one thing Croiset always admitted he was not so good at was being able to provide information about the perpetrators of crimes. It wasn't until more than ten years later that the driver who had given the two girls their ride that unfortunate night was given a life sentence—for the sexually related murder of another young woman.

detailed description of his daughter's movements since her disappearance and predicted she would be in touch within six days. On the sixth day, the professor went downstairs to find his daughter sitting on the living-room couch, safe and sound.

Heading East

Going to Japan, in May 1976, Croiset allegedly saw a television program about a seven-year-old schoolgirl, Miwa Kikuchi, who had been missing for two days. Croiset immediately sensed, from her photograph, that she was dead and that her body was floating on a lake. He drew a map and led investigators to the spot—where the little girl's body was found, precisely as he had described it would be.

Even the skeptical Stephen Peterson, writing in *Psychic Sleuths*, concludes: "Croiset's celebrated career as a paragnost is unique in the modern era, in that no other psychic detective can quite match his reputation or the long period of success he enjoyed." Yet the debate continues over how reliable Croiset's most ardent supporter was when he recorded the psychic's involvement in cases. Was Professor Tenhaeff an impartial archivist or does his close relationship with Croiset make his documentation questionable?

GRETA ALEXANDER: THE HOMELY PSYCHIC

"My life changed one stormy spring night in 1961, when I was struck by lightning. That night I was given the gift of clairvoyance, clairsensory, and clairaudience. I dreamt I was reading the lines in the hand. Over the past 36 years, I have aided police officers in finding hundreds of missing persons. I have been doing ongoing research in hand analysis and medicine. I've had three live radio shows and a cable television program with topics of how to become in tune with yourself."

So begins the website dedicated to Greta Alexander (http://www.gretaalexander.com/story.htm), one of America's best-loved and best-known psychics. It also makes extraordinary claims such as "Did you know Greta could see cancer and other ailments in your hand? It's true." The site also has an impressive list of awards and recommendations from police departments, civil authorities, and members of the public for her work in crime fighting.

Sadly, Alexander died in 1998, but before her death you could be forgiven for believing she was one of the few psychic detectives who had unequivocally been proven to be genuine, because she received so much positive publicity.

Police praise Alexander

An Associated Press story, dated November 6, 1985, has the convincing headline: "Psychic's Description of Missing Man and Death Scene Proves Accurate." The story details how Alexander's advice was "sought by police," after the disappearance of car mechanic Ronald Dean Hicks, in Harrisburg, Illinois. At the request of Hicks's wife, police asked Alexander to help on the case after they had exhausted their leads.

Sheriff Harry Spiller of Williamson County, Illinois, reported Alexander had predicted over the telephone that Hicks was dead, and that he had been shot twice. She also told the police the body would be found "near a bridge and a pool of smelly water along a patch used by hunters." The body of this missing man was found on November 2, 1985, in circumstances so similar to the psychic's predictions that the sheriff told journalists, "It's real weird, to be truthful. I've never seen anything like this before."

Alexander was a popular and easy-to-spot figure in Illinois. She generated much media attention in the area, and her work with local charities made her well-loved, and something of a tourist attraction. As with many psychic detectives, she did not make any money from her work with the police, so she used her talent in other ways to make a living. Requiring two offices and various assistants to organize her busy schedule, Alexander offered private readings to bring in some cash, thus following a long tradition among psychics, mediums, and fortune-tellers.

For $40 per half hour, she "read" palms, after her clients first produced a print of their hand so that she could study the finer lines. Alexander had many admirers and the waiting list for a sitting could be as long as nine months! She even attracted celebrity clients, including Debbie Reynolds and Ruth Warrick, the actress from TV soap opera *All My Children*.

RIGHT: Greta Alexander defied all preconceptions about how a psychic sleuth should look or behave.

A thriving business

Greta's great talent was locating missing people, particularly, it seems, if water was involved. Authors Marcello Truzzi and Arthur Lyons begin their book, *The Blue Sense*, with one of Alexander's most famous cases, that of the murder of Mary L. Cousett, and reporters who visited her toward the end of her life said it wasn't unusual if the constant telephone calls contained ten or more requests a week from police departments seeking advice.

It is highly unusual for the police to openly praise the usefulness of a psychic on an investigation, not least because of the existing preconception that

ABOVE: Actress Debbie Reynolds is believed to have been so impressed with Alexander's psychic intuition, that she became one of her regular clients.

second sight is somehow akin to witchcraft. Alexander herself has been open to some criticism, and one state attorney from Madison County in Illinois forbade his forces from using her services again, saying he was a Christian and her practices, no matter whether they were accurate or not, were occult.

Alexander's list of official supporters is quite extraordinary, though. Retired Captain Arif Mosrie, a former chief of the homicide division of Washington, D.C. Police Department, told *The Winnipeg Sun* that "Greta Alexander has got extraordinary psychic powers—and that is a fact," after Alexander helped in the capture of a man who raped and then strangled his victim. Detective William Fitzgerald from Alton, Illinois, told reporters he was "skeptical to begin with, but I guess I am going to have to be a believer now," after Alexander gave twenty-two accurate psychic impressions in the Cousett case. Polk County, Iowa, Sheriff's Deputy John Hampel, who worked on a case of a missing woman from Iowa, told Max D. Isaacson in *Fate* magazine that Alexander was incredible. "It's an unexplained power she has," he said. "When I first considered using a psychic, other members of the department kidded me about it. So I thought 'to hell with them,' and I went home and phoned her on my own. Afterward, because the information she gave me made some sense, others started to pay some attention to her too." These are just three of the many hundreds of official cases Alexander claimed to work on throughout her life.

The lightning-bolt psychic

Alexander's gift appeared when she was pregnant with her fifth child and lying in bed, staring out of a window and watching a thunderstorm. All of a sudden the bedroom was hit by lightning and the bed was set alight. Alexander and her unborn child were unharmed, but

BELOW: Many psychics claim their powers are triggered by an accident, often a blow to the head. In Alexander's case, her gift materialized after her house was struck by lightning.

from that moment, Alexander seemed to know when the phone was going to ring and who would be on the other end. The "gift" was overseen by two spirit guides called Raoul and Isaiah, whom she referred to as "my boys," and who she credited with helping her receive the right information about people.

Alexander often talked of giving up her police work, not because she didn't get paid for it, or because the resulting publicity tended to provide fuel for the skeptics, but because it was so physically draining. She said she often "became" the missing person or victim for a while, and she actually relived their pain and suffering, and that is how she could tell what had happened and where they were.

Alexander used to say she had flashes, or visions which were a bit like a flickering TV screen, where events would be played out that let her help someone she wanted to tune in to. These were enhanced by her interest in palmistry and the knowledge she said her guides gave her. Alexander also took note of astrological charts, which she said helped her pinpoint information about a particular person.

Yet, Alexander kept working on crime cases because of the many acknowledgments she received. These included headlines such as *The Winnipeg Sun's*

BELOW: As the lightning hit Alexander's window, she saw a radiant image of a an angel. Since that day, she continued to have angelic visions, believing her psychic gift was from God.

The Body by the Bridge

Mary L. Cousett was twenty-eight years old when she went missing from her hometown of Alton, Illinois, on April 24, 1983. The police immediately suspected her boyfriend Stanley Holliday, Jnr., and he was arrested. Although there seemed little doubt Cousett had been murdered, without a body the police had to release Holliday. Seven months after her disappearance the police were no nearer locating Cousett, until someone decided to contact the well-known psychic Greta Alexander.

Alexander drew a circle on a map of the area where she said the body would be located. Although the police had already combed the site, she insisted they would find the body there. She made a whole string of predictions, most notably that the body would be uncovered without the head and without "a leg or a foot," that the letter "S" was significant, and that the body would be located by a man with a deformed hand. Sure enough, as Truzzi and Lyons report in The Blue Sense, "the skull was found five feet from the body, the left foot was missing, and the auxiliary policeman who found the body, Steve Trew, had a deformed left hand, the result of an accident."

All in all, twenty-two of Alexander's predictions were publicized by the police department as being helpful in the case, and Detective William Fitzgerald went on record with many news organizations saying that he was astonished by how accurate the psychic was.

In Psychic Sleuths: ESP and Sensational Cases, edited by Joe Nickell, investigative reporter Ward Lucas examines the Cousett case in detail, including reinterviewing the then-retired Detective Fitzgerald. In a United Press International story dated three days after Cousett's body was found, Fitzgerald was quoted as saying "I was skeptical to begin with, but I guess I'm going to have to be a believer now." Yet, according to Lucas, after the case died down, the detective began to have his doubts—after all, the body wasn't even discovered in the circled area that the psychic had drawn on the map. Out of the twenty-two clues he has reexamined, he can explain away twenty-one of them as being so vague or general that they were bound to fit—only the "deformed hand" still niggles him. He told Lucas that that prediction "still blows my mind."

"We Believe in Her: Police" on March 31, 1983, and letters of recommendation such as the one from the village of Shorewood Police Department in Illinois dated March 12, 1993, which says, "On behalf of Chief Donald R. Lattin and myself, I would like to thank you for your valuable assistance to the Duvall case. Your assistance has made a positive contribution to this case and is greatly appreciated."

One of the more spectacular of Alexander's cases was the missing student Ramon DiVirgilio. The young student, from Des Moines, Iowa, had apparently tried to swim across a swollen river and had got into trouble. The police were sure DiVirgilio was dead, but they were unable to find a body. According to reports, they asked Alexander to help. Although the boy had already been missing for seven weeks, she felt she could provide some information for the police.

While Sergeant Dave Davis walked along the riverbank on June 12, 1979, Alexander was on the telephone relaying her psychic impressions to another police officer who kept in contact with Davis. Although it seemed a long shot, she told the sergeant where to walk and started telling him what he would be able to see. Chief Robert Brunk told the Associated Press reporter that the psychic had said "He's very very close now. He's there," when Davis had radioed that he had come to a bridge. When he waded into the water, a body was found under the bridge. The body was later identified as the unfortunate student. The Associated Press report quoted the Deputy Polk County Medical Examiner, Dr. Dale Grunewald as saying, "It was incredible."

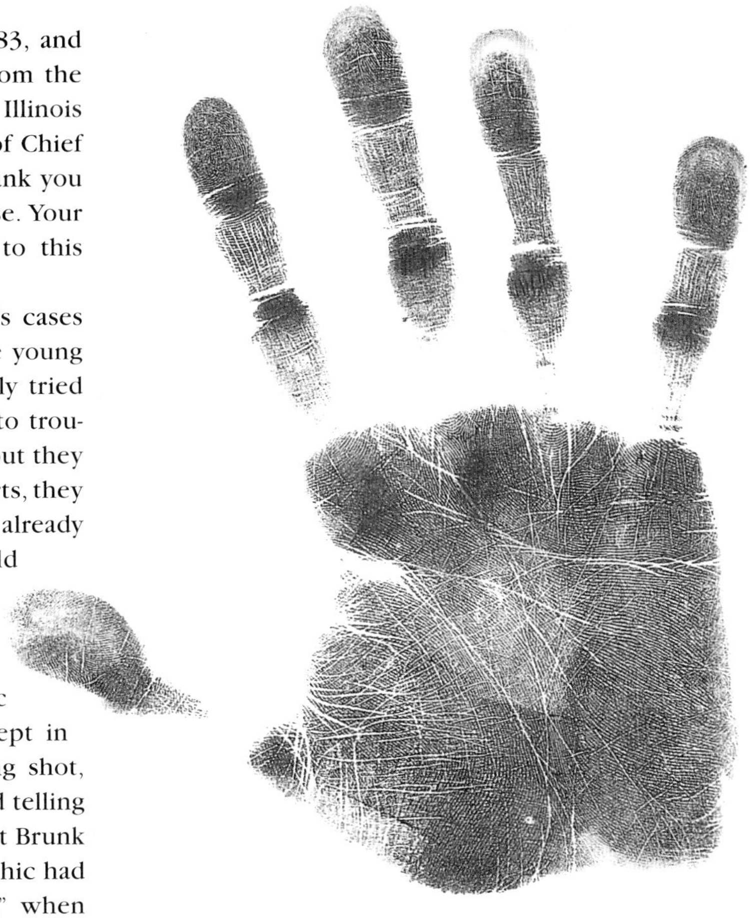

ABOVE: When she wasn't working on police cases, Alexander gave palm readings, often working from a hand print. She could allegedly diagnose illnesses from the lines in the hand.

The healing hands

Some of Alexander's lesser-known talents involved predicting and potentially helping in healing individuals by diagnosing illnesses from their palm prints. Her own documentation about this work is, according to her authorized Internet site, still in the hands of the courts who are overseeing her will. In the January 1981 issue of *Fate* magazine, however, an article by Max D. Isaacson publicized this line of her psychic ability when the writer talked to two doctors who had worked with her.

Dr. Glen E. Tomlinson and Dr. Leon Curry both told Isaacson they were impressed with Alexander's work. "The two hope to establish that palm and fingerprint reading can be another credible method of making certain diagnoses," Isaacson reported. Tomlinson is quoted as saying about Alexander, "She can pinpoint things intuitively and she has a high degree of accuracy." Alexander told Wes Smith of the *Chicago Tribune* that doctors called her before operations—and "lawyers call her before going to trial and producers call her before picking a cast."

Most of the certificates of achievement which are displayed on the website are from fire departments thanking her for her help. She appeared to have a high success rate, not only involving missing people connected with water, but also at solving crimes for fire departments, such as arson.

Her work, despite appearing very glamorous, was mainly with everyday people. She described herself to Wes Smith as an "Earth Mama," and said, "Baby, I've found everything from false teeth to missing kitty cats." The fact that her house in Delavan, Illinois, became a recognized tourist attraction, and that her offices were listed among the area's more mainstream

businesses in local directories, is testament to how seriously she was taken by those she helped.

A tribute to Alexander's powers came from an unexpected source. In *The Blue Sense*, Truzzi and Lyons examine many of Alexander's cases, saying at one point, "Though every one of her many cases can individually be challenged with possible (if not always plausible) alternative explanations for the results, her good (though far from perfect) record of producing satisfied clients argues strongly that she has something interesting, if not psychic, going for her."

Truzzi went further, telling the *Chicago Tribune*, "I am comfortable in recommending Greta because I don't feel she is going to rip anybody off—she is not trying to make a fast buck at this; in fact, all the evidence seems to go the other way."

VANGA DIMITROVA: THE BLIND PROPHETESS

Vanga Dimitrova had the unique distinction of being publicly acknowledged by her government because of her psychic gift. She died in 1996 (references to her age vary, but it is believed she was in her eighties), and was not only a national institution in her home country of Bulgaria, but her death prompted obituaries around the world. One of the most famous mediums of her time, Dimitrova featured in Bulgarian tourist guides, and a hotel even had to be opened near her Petrich home to accommodate her many clients.

Dimitrova was investigated by numerous scientists, and every time she survived their scrutiny, leaving her examiners unable to explain her extraordinary powers of intuition. She was even tested by Dr. Georgi Lozanov, head of both the Institute of Suggestology in Sofia and the Institute of Parapsychology in Petrich, who concluded that Dimitrova's powers were real, not faked. Lozanov also visited the psychic in her own home, joining the line outside for a reading, without telling Dimitrova who he was. According to Sheila Ostrander and Lynn Schroeder's book *Psychic Discoveries: Behind the Iron Curtain*, Lozanov tried to block the psychic's talent by using all his willpower to imagine that he was someone else. Sure enough, Dimitrova couldn't give him a

LEFT: Vanga Dimitrova, the blind medium whose sixth sense made her a much sought-after figure in her native Bulgaria.

ABOVE: The Communist Party headquarters in Sofia, Bulgaria. It is rumored that Dimitrova's insights were sought by high-ranking Bulgarian and Russian party members.

clear reading, although she guessed his name, and that he was a professor linked to parapsychology who had come to test her. She also predicted they would work together in the future—and they did.

Losing and gaining the power of sight

During her early teens, Dimitrova had suffered brief spells when her sight would fail; then, when she was still only nineteen, Dimitrova became totally blind, despite the best efforts of her family to help her. The nineteen-year-old may have been robbed of the gift of sight, but almost as if in compensation, Dimitrova seemed to have been granted another sense—that of psychic ability, or extrasensory perception.

From then on, Dimitrova worked with an increasing number of her countrymen, more often than not predicting future events, which she seemed to know as if she had people's lifeplans in front of her. She also worked with the Bulgarian police solving crimes, and because she was nationally renowned with some very credible references, the police were less hesitant about using her services. She was also known for finding missing people and was able to allegedly diagnose diseases before they had even been contracted.

A case cited by Ostrander and Schroeder tells of a woman they met while researching the blind prophetess in Bulgaria. The woman told them of her father, a doctor who was also very skeptical of psychic matters, who had gone to see Dimitrova at her house in Petrich. The psychic had told him intimate details about his previous marriages before telling the man he would die in fourteen years' time from cancer. She also predicted his favorite son would die in an accident in his twenties and that his daughter (the woman the authors were talking to) would have a wonderful marriage, but her young husband would die just after their first baby was born. Everything the psychic predicted, including the exact date her father died had, according to the woman, come true.

Dimitrova seemed to be very accurate at pinpointing dates of death, and although people did not necessarily want to know them, and the knowledge seemed

ABOVE: The devastation across Europe during World War II meant that Dimitrova's skills were in great demand, as wives and mothers wanted to know if their men would survive.

LEFT: Sadly, Dimitrova knew that one of her own brothers would be killed in the fighting. She predicted his death to the exact day.

to distress her, she generally shared her insights. Her work during World War II, when people visited wanting to know when and if loved ones would return, must have been particularly draining, especially when she "knew" one of her own brothers would not come back. He died on the exact day she predicted, at twenty-three years of age.

As far as the limited information available about her talent goes, it seems Dimitrova was not entirely sure how her powers worked, just that she would receive images of past, present, and future events when she met people. She could also predict future events without any prompting, and famously predicted the imminent arrival of the man she would marry, to her disbelieving sister.

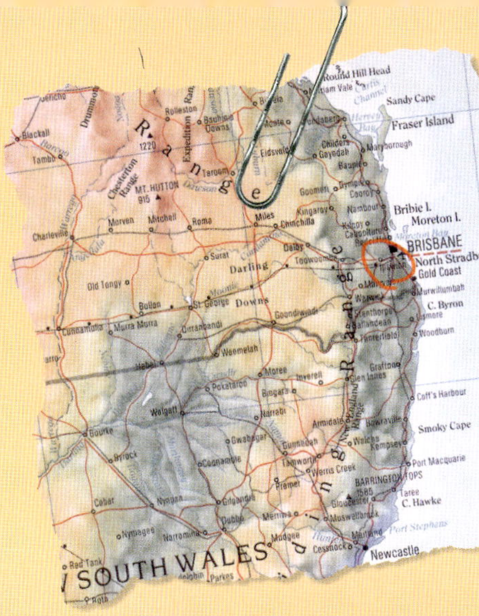

Detecting Down Under

A story printed in the Australian Courier Mail on February 6, 1992, was headlined "Psychic Tells Police of Phillips' Grave Site," and told of how "Homicide detectives will check a world-renowned psychic's belief that the body of Sharron Phillips, missing for nearly six years, is in a shallow grave in a paddock west of Ipswich."

The famed psychic referred to was none other than the blind prophetess Vanga Dimitrova. She didn't travel to the site herself, but sent an assistant, who brought back a watch belonging to the girl, and some photographs of the area where the girl went missing. The psychic, whom the paper reported as "described by European scientists as the best in her field" gave the Australian police a map and marked one of the photographs with the exact spot of the body. She also detailed various markers nearby and said that the woman would be found face down in her grave.

Monitored by the government

After the death of her husband, Dimitrova carried on her work helping people, and continued to have long lines waiting outside her home. Her fame, though, meant she had two secretaries to arrange appointments and record her predictions so they could be checked. Her accuracy rating was described by scientists at about eighty percent, which means, although not right all the time, her "gift" cannot have been pure guesswork. The state tourist board took reservations for sittings with the famous psychic, and the hotel near her home provided visitors with sugar lumps, which they would then place under their pillows as they slept and take with them for Dimitrova to "read" the following morning. It is alleged that even members of the government and various celebrities visited the psychic for help, not just ordinary people with everyday problems.

In Ostrander and Schroeder's follow-up work, *Psychic Discoveries: The Iron Curtain Lifted*, they say that before Dimitrova died she gave away her secret, telling people her power came, following a long tradition of mediums, from the spirits of the dead who came with people when they visited her. Dimitrova believed she was aided by those who had already passed away.

BELOW: An unusual form of psychometry, Dimitrova "read" sugar lumps that had been placed under the client's pillow at night. She alleged the cubes absorbed the person's energy.

SHERIFF
PRIDE OF TEXAS
COUNTY

CHAPTER THREE

Unconventional Wisdom

The Police and Psychic Detection

Someone, somewhere today will be offering a police force information about a crime, gained they believe through psychic powers. Generally, the police will have a set policy on how to deal with such information. It is usually filed away and forgotten.

But some of the people who have psychic visions, premonitions, or clues presented to them, aren't dismissed politely when they contact the police, even in today's hi-tech crime-solving world of DNA profiling and internationally linked police headquarters. Some individuals are considered, from their track records, too important not to take seriously, and it is these people who provide the most interesting evidence that psychic abilities can be used in crime detection and prevention work.

The picture is far more complex than the stereotypical idea of the traditional "mystic" woman poring over her crystal ball or going into trance. Today's psychic detectives come in all shapes and forms, from homely housewives to the more media-friendly, polished PR person.

Hardly any of these psychic detectives charge more than basic expenses for their efforts. Some have to restrict the amount of work they take on because it is so emotionally draining, and some only work anonymously because they are afraid of reprisals. Helping the police can be unforgiving work—police departments are understandably reluctant to publicly admit they work with psychics and, therefore, sometimes don't even bother to inform the individual how accurate they were (or weren't!).

Families can also put a strain on the psychic detective. Desperate to hear news of loved ones, their suffering can put a huge responsibility onto the psychic, turning them into more of a counselor than an investigator. This is why most psychics choose only to work directly with the police.

The psychic detectives discussed in this chapter all have connections with police forces, and their descriptions of how their talent works and why they do what they do are fascinating. Most put up with the skepticism leveled at them from certain quarters and are generally aware of the damage their unpredictable sixth sense can cause. In fact, more than one psychic detective has suggested it would be an excellent idea to regulate their work.

The February 1979 edition of the *Criminal Information Bulletin* contained a paper from the Californian Department of Justice titled "Use of Psychics in Law Enforcement." The simple fact that a department of justice was willing to examine the topic seemed revolutionary, especially for something written over two decades ago.

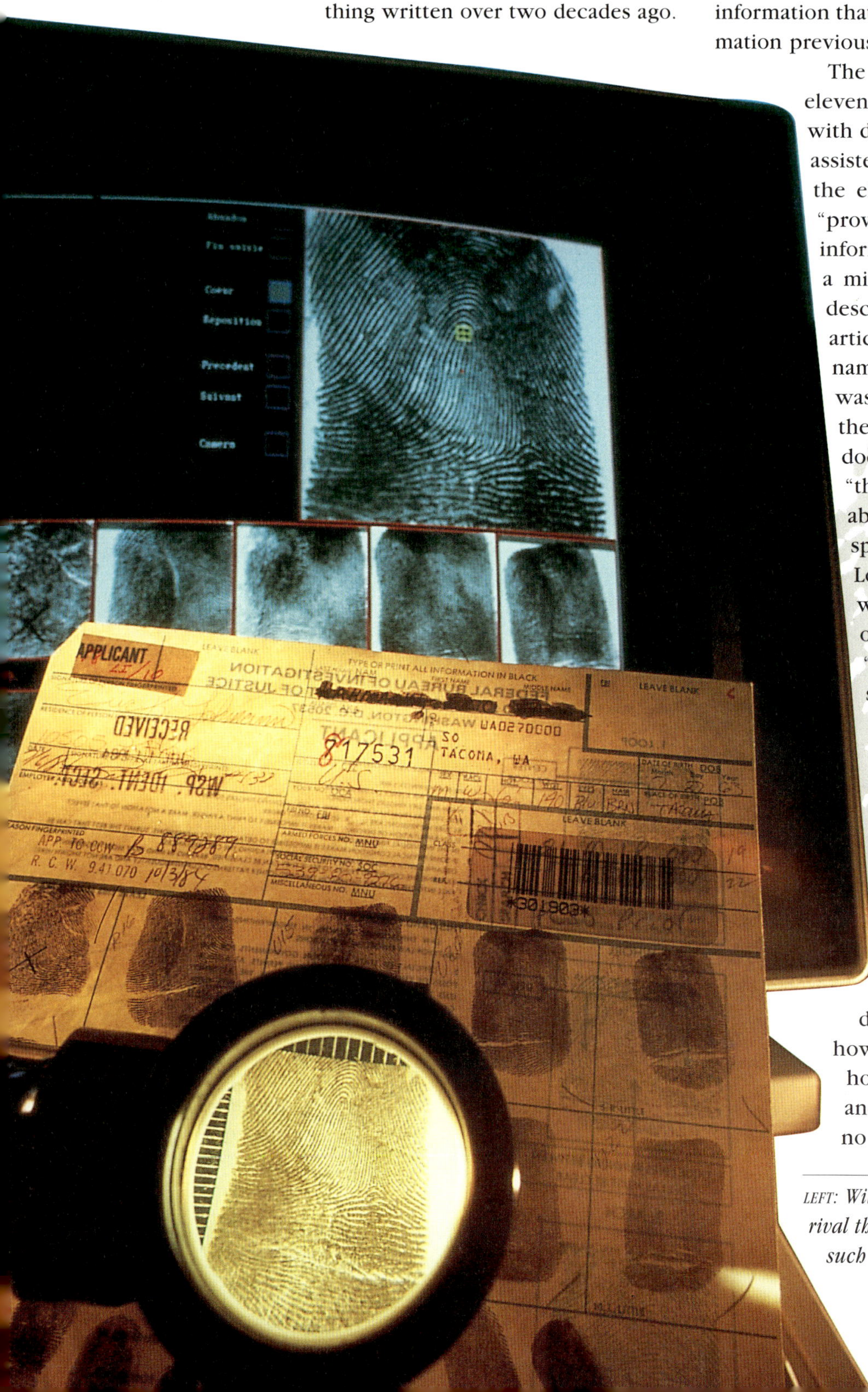

The Californian research, published to inform local officers, is even more interesting because it concludes: "Based upon this survey, it would appear that a talented psychic can assist you by helping to: locate a geographical area of a missing person; narrow the number of leads to be concentrated on; highlight information that has been overlooked; or provide information previously unknown to the investigator."

The survey was conducted by interviewing eleven police officers who had been involved with different cases where psychics had also assisted with the investigation. Eight out of the eleven reported that the psychics had "provided them with otherwise unknown information," and in three of the eight cases a missing body was found at the location described by the psychic. Although the article doesn't go into the specific cases, or name the four psychics whose information was used by the police, the outcome of the report is, nevertheless, positive. "It does appear," the report's author writes, "that some psychics have provided valuable assistance to law enforcement on specific cases." It also mentions that the Los Angeles Police Department (LAPD) was in the process of conducting its own study, which would hopefully be "another indication of the overall success rate that might be expected from psychics."

When the LAPD report was finally published later in 1979, the overall conclusion was that psychics were no more likely to provide useful information than anyone else. The official policy of the LAPD is that they don't employ psychic detectives.

So what are we to make of this confusion, where some police departments are offering advice on how to choose a psychic detective and how best to interpret their information, and yet others publicly state they have no interest in the phenomenon? More

LEFT: Will psychically divined criminal profiles ever rival the everyday tools of police investigation, such as digitized fingerprint records?

ABOVE: The LAPD on patrol. Their official policy is that psychics are no more likely to help an investigation than any other member of the public offering information.

than twenty years after an important state department issued guidelines which seemed to advocate employing psychics to help on certain cases, why is the area still so controversial?

The police only tend to speak publicly about involving psychic detectives with their work when either the family involved has requested a psychic's presence, or when the police really have run out of leads and ideas. Interestingly, most psychic detectives don't work on cases unless they have been specifically asked by the family or the officers involved, otherwise they find their information is either ignored, or used but they aren't credited for it.

There are, however, some very good reasons why psychics are not generally trusted by police forces. Admittedly, a few American forces have gone on record saying that information provided by psychics was useful, but few advocate actually seeking the help of second sight detectives. Certainly, the British police are still extremely skeptical when it comes to dealing with information from psychics. Even the one and only publicly recognized British police officer who also claims to be psychic, Keith Charles of the Surrey Constabulary, says phone calls and information from supposed psychics are listened to politely, but that far too many provide useless information.

Needing facts not fiction

The main problem the police have with information provided by psychics, apart from the fact that evidence inspired by extrasensory perception (ESP) is not permissible in court, is that it appears to need careful interpretation. A psychic will tend to get a vision of a crime, not a list of names and addresses, and that vision occurs in flashes, which can well be from different perspectives and even different time periods.

Skeptics argue that psychics offer such vague clues as "near water," or "my head hurts," or "there are children involved" because these broad "guesses" have a good chance of being close to something on the case. Usually, the psychic's usefulness is evaluated only after a crime has been solved, and, skeptics say, gullible

ABOVE: *Suspicion has often surrounded those who claim to have psychic powers. As recently as 1944, British medium Helen Duncan was imprisoned under the Witchcraft Act.*

police and vulnerable families then desperately fit these vague clues to something—perhaps anything—linked to the case.

So, the evidence for psychic ability when it comes to the world of crime, according to skeptics, comes from three highly unreliable sources: Firstly, the psychics themselves; secondly, police officers who have been taken in by the psychics; and thirdly, by families and friends of victims who are simply being deceived.

The fact that most psychic detectives don't ask for payment for their services, hasn't totally protected them from the wrath of skeptics. The two main arguments against what they purport to do, are that it wastes public money when police spend time following fruitless leads, and it cruelly gives families false hopes.

A 1987 report published in the British journal *Police Review*, looked at the case of the murder of a girl named Sarah Jane Harper. As with most high-profile child murders, police received lots of offers of

When the Psychics get it Wrong

Although there has never been a psychic detective who claimed to get it right 100 percent of the time, certain cases have undoubtedly had their critics, especially when the families involved have been subjected to unnecessary trauma.

Many psychic detectives have publicly condemned other so-called psychics who set themselves up with expensive telephone charge lines and dupe the public into believing they are for real. Psychics Nancy Myer and Noreen Renier, for example, told authors Truzzi and Lyons they would welcome some sort of official regulation for their work.

It is not always bad news, though. American psychic Phil Jordan was brought in on a 1975 case of a missing boy aged five. The child had wandered off near Empire Lake, in Spencer, New York. The police had searched the whole area where the child had last been seen and Jordan was called in as a last resort because he had worked on a previous missing person case.

Jordan immediately sensed that the boy was alive and well, and this was after seventeen hours of searching by the police. Jordan drew a map of the area where he thought the boy would be and told police he was asleep under a tree. He was found exactly as Jordan had predicted, in an area that was uncannily similar to the map.

The case received widespread coverage and has often been cited as one of the most successful examples of psychic location work, yet, there have been cases where psychics have been unforgivably wrong. One of the dangers of bringing in a psychic on investigations involving missing children, is that frantic parents will, of course, be desperate to know if their children are alive. An example is the case of Brian Timmerman, an American boy who had been missing for over a month when Dorothy Allison (see page 41-7) got involved in the case. She told police he had suffocated and was dead. Her other clues didn't help the police, but Timmerman was eventually found alive and well selling leaflets and paraphernalia for the Moonies in New York City. Speculation that the psychic thought the boy was dead, because he could have been considered so in the spiritual sense, would be poor consolation for his distraught parents.

ABOVE: The murder of Sarah Jane Harper shocked the British public and led to 600 psychics offering information to the police.

RIGHT: A painting, supposedly depicting the man responsible for Sarah Jane's death, was sent anonymously to the Yorkshire Post *newspaper. It was not too dissimilar to the police artist's sketch of the suspect. Could this be a psychic's impression?*

help from psychics—in this case, 600 separate offers to be exact! The report calculated that it would have taken about six hours for a police officer to assess each psychic's contribution, which would have meant a total of 3,600 hours to sift through all the psychic clues.

The psi price to pay

Estimating that not only detectives would be involved, but that the information would need to be coordinated from a control room, requiring an additional 1,200 working hours, the total budgetary cost based on an average of £7.00 an hour worked out at a massive £34,000—and that was for just evaluating the information, not following it up.

But expenses aren't the only factor to consider when the police are at a loss to find the killer of a child and all conventional avenues have been explored. The family involved is likely to want to try anything and to them £34,000 is nothing. To them, sifting through 600 different psychic "visions" could just lead to one being right ... perhaps the skeptics are right to be concerned about the heartbreak so-called ESP may cause.

The Californian Department of Justice have stated they don't use just any psychics, only ones with a proven track record. In *The Blue Sense*, authors Marcello Truzzi and Arthur Lyons cite the case of Californian psychic Dixie Yeterian, who was conducting a live phone-in on her local radio station in 1978 when a teenage boy called asking for details of his missing father. The boy, Owen Etheridge, sounded inconsolable, and Yeterian told him to bring various objects that

The Williston Case

ABOVE: Businesswoman Noreen Renier did not believe in psychic powers—until she discovered her own.

On March 24, 1994, a sixty-six-year-old man named Norman Lewis left his house in Williston, Florida, in his truck and simply disappeared. He left behind his wallet and various personal items, which he would have been expected to take if he was going on a long trip. The case baffled the local police. Williston is a small town, and the police initially thought this would be a simple case which would be cleared up relatively quickly.

Despite hundreds of leads, after two years the police and Lewis's family were nowhere nearer finding out what had happened to him. It was at this point that the family suggested the police contact a psychic detective.

Luckily for the family, Detective Brian Hewitt, who worked with the Williston police, had recently attended a conference where psychic detective Noreen Renier had lectured. Hewitt was impressed by Renier and decided to recommend her services to the Lewis family. Because it was outside the ordinary parameters of police work, the family paid Renier for her psychic services.

When Detective Hewitt telephoned Renier she agreed straight away to help. The police had not progressed the case for more than two years, so it was felt her involvement couldn't do any harm, and she wasn't going to be accused of wasting police time. Hewitt made an appointment and visited Renier in Orlando, Florida.

Renier was sent two personal items belonging to the missing man—his wallet and a shoe. She began work on the case at once, although certain critics have argued she didn't start until three weeks after hearing about the investigation. This, they say, would have given the psychic plenty of time to research the history of the case and also the geography of the area involved.

Renier has spoken about her involvement, pointing out that even if she did "cheat," which she says she never does, it wouldn't have helped find Norman Lewis: "When I work on a case, I don't want to know anything about it except is it a homicide or a missing person. I never even ask for the name of the victim. As a psychic, I use my intuitive mind to get the answers." Even if she had gathered together all the facts in the case, she wouldn't have learned any more than the police already knew and they were no nearer to finding out the answer to the mystery than they had been when Lewis disappeared.

When Renier sat down with the wallet and the shoe, she didn't know whether their owner was alive or dead, but she says the images started coming almost immediately, "one after the other." She relived what had happened both from the point of view of an eyewitness and as if she was Norman Lewis. She saw Lewis in his truck and "watched" as it veered off a road and went down a cleft. Renier told the police she knew Lewis had had an accident and also that he was dead. She was also able to give them vital clues which helped in locating the body: "I told them the

"Without Noreen Renier we would not have located Norman Lewis. I'm extremely impressed with her abilities. She told us things that she would have to have been an eyewitness to have known."
Olin Slaughter, Chief of Police, Williston P.D., Williston Pioneer, June 27, 1996.

mileage from his [Lewis's] house (2.1 miles), the number of a road (44), the other clues I could see were that he would be found in his truck, the still water, the bricks, the railroad tracks, a bridge, the clefts, and the weeds above me when I was Lewis in the truck."

As soon as Renier presented her information to the Williston Police Department, officers put together her clues and started work looking for what they now believed would be a body. There turned out to be several areas of water that distance from Lewis's home, but when navy divers searched a lake-filled local limestone quarry along State Route 45 (Renier's prediction of a road numbered 44 had come very close), they found Lewis's truck under weeds in the murky water, with his body inside. The local police force made public statements to the media about the success of Renier's predictions and the discovery of the body hit newspaper headlines throughout the United States.

As with all these cases, the facts are not always as they seem. Skeptics have had a field day trying to find holes in the case, yet despite all their protestations, they cannot argue with the fact that it wasn't until the family requested the involvement of a psychic, that the mystery surrounding Norman Lewis was solved. It is embarrassing for a highly trained police team to admit they have run out of clues on a case—and even more embarrassing to admit that a woman who calls herself psychic actually helped them locate a body they hadn't been able to find for two years, despite modern policing methods.

As Renier says, "if logic could have been used to find Mr. Lewis, or solve unsolved police cases, they would not need me. All the local police and I'm sure half the town were looking for him."

When the police located the body, the family of the deceased man phoned Renier and was, according to the psychic, "extremely grateful." She had ended more than two years of uncertainty.

Talking about how she receives her unique insight, Renier says she doesn't really do anything special. She sometimes meditates and occasionally likes a glass of wine to relax, but then the images "come from my mind, which somehow has focused on the energies of that individual at that particular time. I'm in another state of consciousness so I can't really describe how it feels, except for the pain, of course, it feels like the pain the person felt."

BELOW: Renier's uncanny prediction, which led police to the missing body, made headlines nationally in the United States.

The Gainesville Sun
Thursday, April 4, 1996

REGION
Classified
Section B

HEMPFEST DEFENDANT LOSE
FIGHT OVER CONSTITUTIONAL
OF MARIJUANA LAWS

Psychic leads police to body

■ The remains inside the truck may belong to a missing Williston man.

By KAREN VOYLES
Sun staff writer

WILLISTON ...
psychic, ...

set of skeletal remains the psychic had assured them would be with the truck ...
"We feel like this is probably ... but we won't ...

KAREN VOYLES
... where to look to find ... ce led Navy divers to ... County limerock pit.

Psychic leads Navy divers to remains of missing man

Civilian divers had searched the pit earlier but had been unable to find anything.

Associated Press

JACKSONVILLE — Navy Chief Warrant Officer Reubin Thornton and his team are trained to find underwater weapons and sunken aircraft, but this time they were searching for a pickup in a water-filled quarry.

The divers were at the quarry at the request of police in Williston. Authorities in the town southwest of Gainesville had been looking for a man missing for two years.

The divers were working on a lead given to police nine months ago by a psychic, who suggested the missing man could be found in a watery grave near home. The psychic was right.

On the second day of searching Wednesday, the six members of Explosive Ordinance Detection Mobile Unit 6 from Mayport Naval Station, near Jacksonville, used an underwater metal detector dragged by boat to find a large object about 30 feet from shore in about 20 feet of water.

Police divers then spent an hour ripping through a thick layer of growth that covered the pickup and the skeletal remains it held.

What Thornton didn't know at the time was that the information the Williston Police Department had on a possible location of Norman Lewis, 76, and his Chevrolet pickup came from Orlando psychic Noreen Renier.

The huge L-shaped limestone quarry was about 1,000 yards by 2,000 yards, Thornton said.

Civilian divers had searched the pit earlier but had been unable to find anything.

"Our equipment is pretty good," Thornton said. He said grass up to five feet long covered the vehicle, making it invisible in the murky water.

The truck and the remains were taken to Gainesville to be examined by Dr. William Maples, a University of Florida forensic anthropologist, and Dr. William Hamilton, the medical examiner, for a positive identification.

Using dental records, they confirmed Thursday that the skeletal remains were those of Lewis, who was last seen March 24, 1994.

After police unsuccessfully tracked down hundreds of leads and spent hours on aerial searches of the area, the Lewis family turned to Ms. Renier.

"She led us to the site, she gave us a lot of clues," Williston Police Chief Olin Slaughter said Thursday. Williston police investigator Brian Hewitt had seen the woman at a police conference, and gave her name to the Lewis family.

On July 17, 1995, Ms. Renier held a piece of Lewis' clothing, then stated a number of details about the retired Navy man, as well as where police should look for him and his truck.

belonged to his father to her after her show, promising she would try to help Etheridge find him.

When the boy turned up at the station, together with his father's watch and a ring, the psychic sleuth held the objects and allegedly "saw" that the son had shot his father in the head. She quickly got rid of Owen, telling him that she couldn't help, and immediately contacted a local homicide detective with whom she had worked before.

The police in this instance knew Yeterian and decided to confront the young boy. The psychic was right; the boy confessed, and the body of his father was located in circumstances also seen by Yeterian when she held his watch.

Mel Ramos, the detective involved, told the authors "we used Dixie on more than one occasion." This was a case where only one psychic was involved, and the police had nothing to lose by spending a little time. In high profile cases, however, when the police have run out of leads, is it worth them approaching psychics, even if they are well known?

BELOW: Blood-stained clothing provides a DNA profile; this technique was only accepted in British courts as recently as 1987. Could psychic insight one day also be used as evidence?

Lorne Mason, a researcher into the paranormal with a special interest in psychic detectives, told writer Andrew Donkin that she believes the police shouldn't dismiss what psychics have to offer and "their skills should be used like the specialist talents of any other outside expert." She also says the police shouldn't totally rely on psychic detectives and that common sense on the part of the officers should play a big part in solving a crime.

The unpredictability of ESP

Psychics don't come more famous than Uri Geller. He has an international reputation that would be hard to duplicate. He has also been tested by numerous research establishments, none of which have declared him a fake. He talks about solving crimes in *The Geller Effect*, his autobiography, but admits to not being particularly good at it. The information he tends to receive is incidental, rather than the crucial facts.

"Why had my powers," he writes, "led me to the exact spot at the right time … and then let me down when it came to the information that really mattered? This kind of thing seems to happen again and again when I am dealing with dangerous people, whether kidnappers or murderers. Are my survival instincts

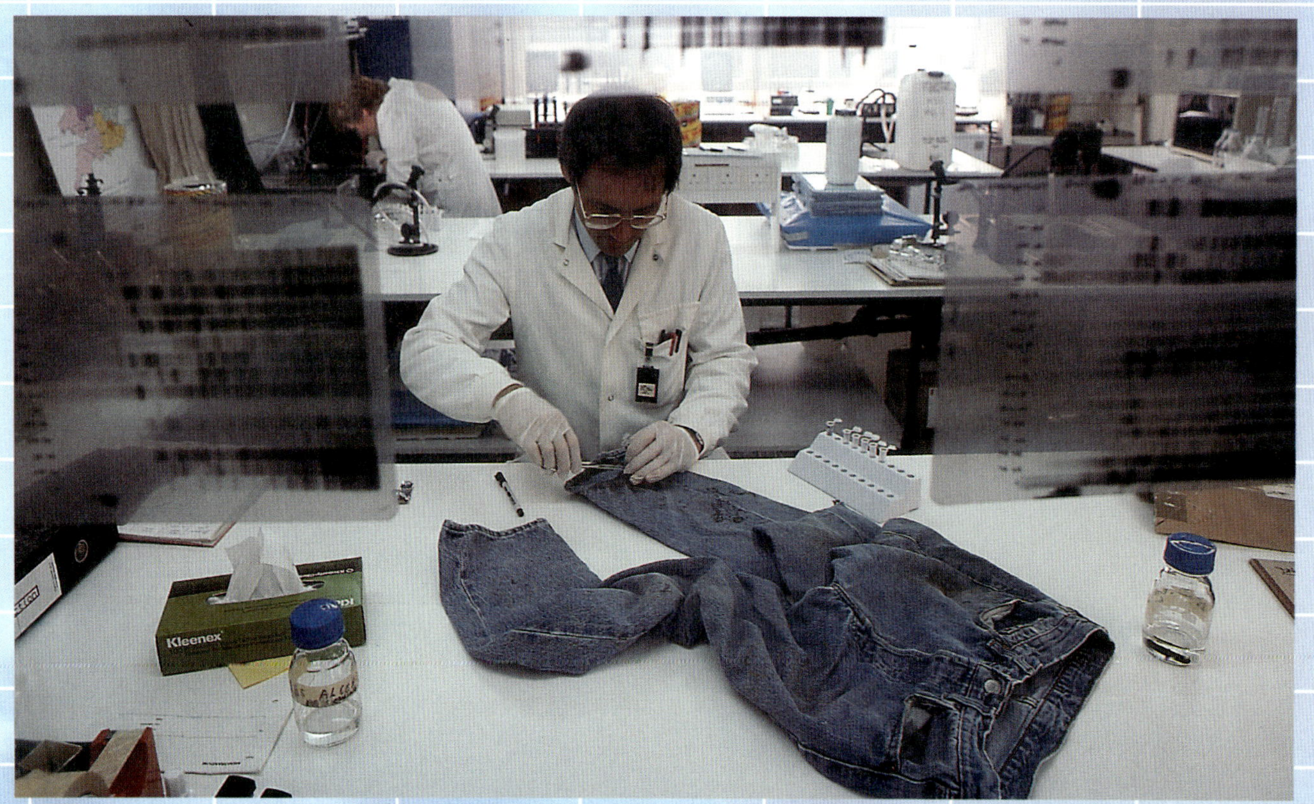

The International Crime Scene

Although it seems the United States has the highest concentration of working psychic detectives, perhaps this is because the country is so vast and has a highly polished media industry. Other countries throughout the world have their own psychic superstars who are known for helping their own police forces with difficult cases.

Dina Nazarenko is Moscow's working psychic detective, having received considerable interest from her home media. Jan Steers, a Dutch psychic detective following in the tradition of countrymen Gerard Croiset and Peter Hurkos, traveled to the United States in the 1970s to help on various cases. Once, according to authors Lyons and Truzzi, he became a suspect because his knowledge of the crime was so accurate it was highly suspicious.

Greece, Sweden, and Jamaica have had psychics who have worked with their own police forces, and even more interesting, it seems working psychics from the United States are now being invited to visit other countries. Riley G. has visited Japan; Noreen Renier was invited to Hong Kong and has worked in Mexico and Canada; even Dorothy Allison, the New Jersey housewife, has worked on cases as far away as Switzerland and Venezuela.

somehow suppressing my psychic ones?"

Geller speculates it is in his own interests that he doesn't use his powers to solve major crimes, because he would be on "every hit-list in the world of organized crime."

Nancy Myer (previously Czetli), an American psychic who says she has been working with police since 1974, and only works with them after she is approached for help, is also wary of working on certain cases. In the April 1993 edition of *Fate* magazine, she said, "I will not do cases that are too dangerous; i.e. when the assailant could turn on me after I have 'ranged' the case. I will only work on such a case if no one [the public] knows that I am there."

Greta Alexander (see page 50) didn't like working on murder cases for a different reason. She "experienced" the crime from the victim's point of view, sometimes physically as well as emotionally. The exhaustion, as well as physical pain, was too much of a drain on her own resources and left her feeling weak and unwell.

So what do these public-spirited detectives get out of trying to help the police? Certainly, the majority of would-be psychics who believe they have had premonitions about a high-profile case, such as the above-mentioned Sarah Jane Harper murder, are acting out of

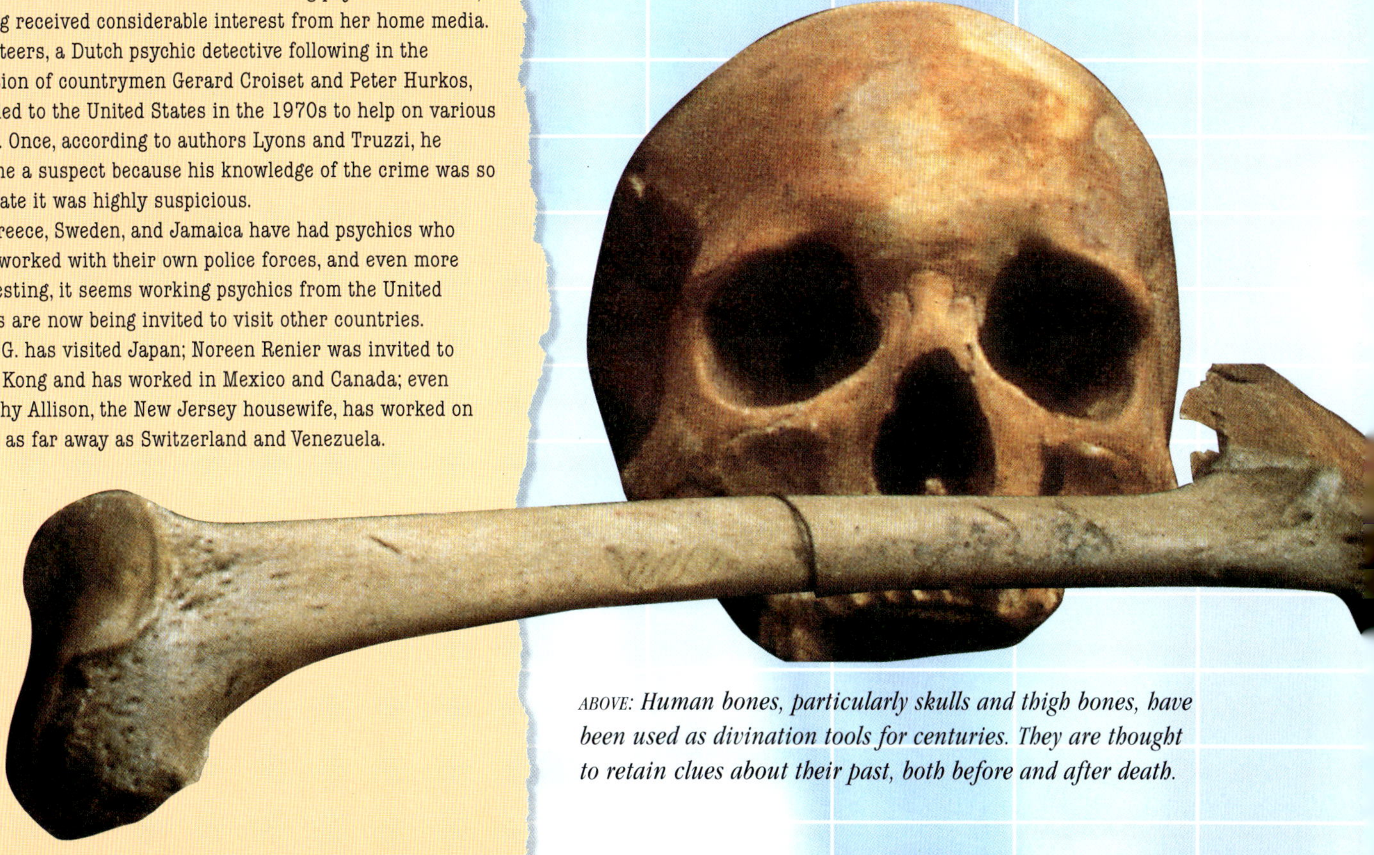

ABOVE: Human bones, particularly skulls and thigh bones, have been used as divination tools for centuries. They are thought to retain clues about their past, both before and after death.

The Green River Serial Killer

ABOVE: *Riley G. conducts corporate training sessions, believing techniques he uses as a psychic, such as self-hypnosis and positive thinking, can benefit other walks of life.*

BELOW: *Working on cases at home and abroad, he is pictured here in Japan, where his powers were tested on a TV show.*

Between 1982 and 1984 in the Seattle-Tacoma area of Washington, the local population lived in fear of a murderer who came to be known as the Green River Serial Killer, because of his habit of leaving his victims near the banks of the Green River, just outside Seattle.

The victims, all young women, were mainly girls who had worked as prostitutes at some time, or were hitchhikers or runaways. It is thought the killer was responsible for approximately forty-eight murders, although there are many more missing young women who fit the profile of the victims on police files. The attacks were sexual in nature. Most of the young women were found either naked or partially clothed, and some were found with foreign objects inserted inside them. Most had been strangled, sometimes with their own underwear.

To date, the killer has not been identified, despite leaving clues at some of the sites and even returning to the bodies on some occasions and dressing them in different clothes. Some commentators believe he enjoyed taunting the police and grew frustrated when they didn't come close to capturing him.

Thirteen years after what were hoped to be the last killings, police were still baffled at how the perpetrator managed to cover his tracks so well. Theories were abundant. Maybe the killer was more than one person, perhaps he had died, or been institutionalized, or even had moved on and was continuing the campaign of terror elsewhere in the United States. Theories are all very well, but to the families of the murdered girls, the heartbreaking mystery of their deaths will remain painfully in the

"I am intrigued by your 'vision' of the killer and would like to hear more. Please feel free to call me ..."

Detective Thomas Jensen, King County Police, Green River Task Force.

open until someone is caught who can answer all their questions.

In 1997, the task force assigned to the case took the unusual step of making contact with Riley G., a psychic detective who was once a New York City cop. Detective Thomas Jensen contacted the psychic on April 9, 1997, and interviewed him about the case.

The detective had become interested in Riley G. after reading about the psychic's visions of the serial killer. During November 1995, Riley G. was interviewed on TV. He was asked to psychically home in on U.S. troop movements in Bosnia, but instead, when he tried to concentrate his thoughts he apparently received information about the Green River case.

"In the initial psychic flashes," he said, "I saw a white male picking up a prostitute. The male was attempting to strangle the female when she pulled out some sort of knife or box cutter and slashed the suspect in the face and arms. The prostitute jumped out of the vehicle and ran away. The suspect shortly thereafter went into hospital and had these severe wounds looked after."

On their own, these "psychic flashes" are limited in their help and could relate to any number of crimes that occur every day, but Riley G. was convinced they were related to the Green River serial murders.

On December 25, 1995, Riley G. was again bombarded with "visions" of the crime, although this time the detail appeared to be specifically related to identifying the killer. Riley G. describes seeing the man as having a "strong physical profile," yet at the time of the murders was on disability leave with back problems. Since that time, Riley G. says he believes the killer's back pain has increased and he may now walk with a stick. The killer still frequents the area, particularly the "strip that the prostitutes were abducted from ... I get the initials A.A. for the suspect's first and last name. The last name may be Archer or something very similar in nature. The suspect is also known to cops who worked in the area during the 1980s, and may well still be known by the cops as I think he still lurks in the night hours."

Riley G.'s vision also showed the killer driving "a green International Scout with a white camper or box extension on the rear of the vehicle." He senses the man had been arrested several times before for assault, probably in connection with prostitutes, and Riley G. also thinks he was a kayaking enthusiast, which is how he gained his detailed knowledge of the Green River.

Riley G. decided to make his information public by posting it on the Internet with a disclaimer saying that he wasn't accusing anyone but only reporting what he had seen in his vision. He is obviously frustrated that the case remains open and unsolved, but is convinced his psychic visions have given a clear picture of the world of a very dangerous serial killer. Hopefully, time will tell whether the police task force was able to use any of Riley G.'s information, and finally reveal the identity of the Green River serial killer ...

ABOVE: The ex-NYPD cop takes time out from his psychic detective work to maintain his own sanity.

a genuine desire to help with information they believe could be valuable. Very few of them make a career as professional psychics, although that isn't necessarily a sign of authenticity.

ABOVE: Doris Stokes often gave stage performances revealing her clairvoyant powers, but most modern psychic detectives see themselves as investigators rather than entertainers.

Desires for fame and fortune?

Doris Stokes, who has to be one of the most famous British mediums of the last century, and one of the most fondly remembered, not only relayed messages for loved ones from their dead relatives, but occasionally, attempted to help police by providing clues to various crimes.

Stokes, who made considerable money from her public appearances and books, has come in for hefty criticism from skeptics such as Ian Wilson, author of several books including *The After Death Experience*. He uncovered examples of deception at her séances, where she had already been in contact with various members of her audience and invited them to the shows so she could demonstrate remarkable knowledge to the rest of the audience. Wilson said that even those people invited to attend by Stokes didn't realize until afterward that the world-famous medium was imparting information from the otherworld that she already knew.

Certainly Stokes' sojourns into detective work haven't been well documented, even in her own books. Facts are often very sketchy, and although she was the darling of the media, when big cases came to light, it is doubtful the police ever took her seriously as an investigative tool.

There are, however, certain "names" who definitely aren't as famous as Stokes, probably because they don't court publicity, but who are consulted by police, or at least taken seriously when their advice is offered. Maybe they only work with private clients, or under assumed names, but they are all using their talents to help either individuals or organizations solve crimes or mysteries.

Night visions

Chris Robinson is not a household name in Britain, although he has published a book, coauthored with journalist Andy Boot. Yet, he has the rare privilege of being asked to work with police, because of his psychic skills. Robinson is Britain's dream detective—

Strange but True

In 1989, psychic Linda Davis, who was used to predicting the future for other people, made the prediction that someone was going to attempt to kill her. That someone was her husband.

Davis, according to researchers Lyons and Truzzi, was known to local police. "She had helped Escondido and San Diego police in several homicide and kidnapping investigations and she had been consulted by law enforcement agencies as far away as Kansas".

A divorce was imminent between Davis and her husband. He had allegedly become threatening and violent toward her, and she had felt the need to buy a gun to protect herself. Her premonition proved correct: On September 10, 1989, she was attacked by her husband. As Davis later said in her statement, he threatened her life and she shot him. The court's verdict was the killing had been self-defense, and Davis was freed.

he "foresees" crimes, particularly those linked to terrorism, while he sleeps.

The foreword to Robinson's book is written by Alex Hall, ex-Detective Chief Inspector with Britain's Regional Crime Squads. Hall was asked by the regional coordinator to monitor Robinson's dreams after the psychic came to their attention in 1988 with information about "an IRA atrocity" about to happen. Hall retired in 1995, so presumably he no longer records Robinson's dreams, but his testimony, although he is careful to point out that he has always used "hard facts and usable evidence," is quite astonishing. He writes, "Chris has been able to offer helpful information in relation to major crimes and terrorist activities," a glowing endorsement considering the attitude of the British police force to psychic phenomena generally.

Robinson says in his book that he has always been psychic, but that the vivid dreams started soon after his first daughter was born. Initially he didn't even record the details of the dreams, or understand what some of the symbols meant (he often gets clues which refer to postcode letters and numbers). Important dreams, which he thinks he should be taking notice of, are generally repeated over a few nights. Robinson now makes notes and even manages to write things down while he is still asleep. If he considers a dream or image important enough, he will contact the police.

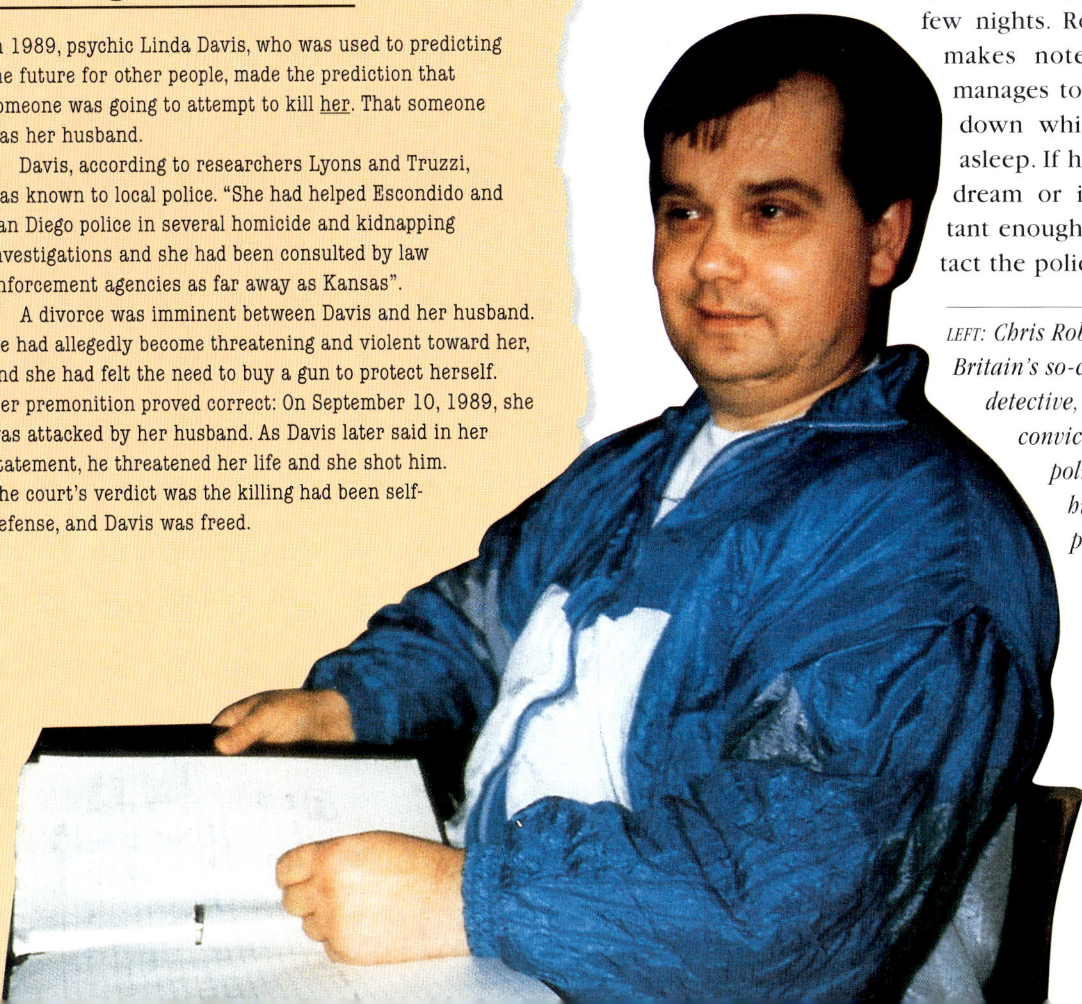

LEFT: Chris Robinson, Britain's so-called dream detective, has won the conviction of the police through his accurate predictions.

The Seven-Eleven Shooting

K.t. Frankovich believes she has been psychic since she was a very young child. She doesn't advertise her abilities but, by word of mouth, many people seem to find her just when they need help. She works with individuals as well as with police departments, helping people with all types of problems. The case of the Seven-Eleven shooting illustrates the problems k.t. says psychics are often faced with when they become involved in areas of crime. Interestingly, the case involves precognition, where k.t. "saw" the crime before it was going to happen. This in itself throws up all sorts of dilemmas for the psychic, but ultimately k.t. was successful in intervening in what was a life-threatening situation.

In 1981, a young woman whom k.t. hadn't met before decided to contact her for a regular reading. As is usual, k.t. was recording their conversation. She remembers asking the girl if she was engaged, and the girl replied that she was, and then all of a sudden, "a premonition began to unfold before my eyes. I could see the explicit details, just as if I was watching the entire event being played out in a filmed sequence."

K.t.'s vision revealed an alarming scenario where the young woman's fiancé drove into the parking lot of a Seven-Eleven store and went inside. The young man was carrying a substantial amount of money. Unbeknown to him, a robbery was taking place inside the store and he was walking straight into it. K.t. saw the young man approach the counter to pay. Two men had their backs to him, but from the look on the store cashier's face, he quickly realized what was going on. The robber nearest the counter was pointing a gun at the cashier, the other robber appeared unarmed but was wearing a jacket. This second man turned and demanded the fiancé turn out his pockets.

ABOVE: K.t. Frankovich believes it is extremely hard to change any course of events, which makes precognition a huge responsibility.

After taking the young man's money, the robber turned his back for a moment and then span around quickly holding a .357-Magnum he'd been hiding. The young man bolted in fear and the gunman fired at point-blank range.

K.t. describes how "the premonition placed me in a very awkward position. I knew what I had seen had been absolutely accurate. I did not know how to communicate it without scaring the daylights out of the young woman sitting beside me, eagerly awaiting to hear the happy news of her future marriage." Believing absolutely in her sixth sense, k.t. was careful to check the tape was working before proving

"About three weeks later, I received a phone call from a Miami police officer. The officer said, 'I had to call to tell you that you saved a young man's life today.' The officer was overwhelmed. In all his years of being on the force, he had never seen anything like this before."

her abilities to the woman by correctly guessing various personal details. She described the woman's fiancé in detail, all the time trying to work out if "her fiancé's behavior could be altered so it was different from that in the premonition … If so, when was the precise, critical moment whereby he might have the opportunity to change the outcome of his destiny?"

Telling the young woman that her boyfriend was going to walk into a robbery, k.t. made her promise that she would make him listen to the tape and memorize every single word. She told the woman that her boyfriend should roll up the money and put it in his sock instead of his coat pocket. Despite the woman's assurances that he never carried such a large sum of money, k.t. says she was convinced he would be at the time the robbery occurred.

Carefully describing the surroundings and situation, k.t. provided a detailed account of how the robbery would take place, hoping that if the young man listened to the tape, he would later recall her words. K.t. says she can replay her visions like "playing a video in a VCR," so she went over and over the moment before the shooting, and realized the young man would be able to see the robber's right hand and arm. As long as he watched that arm and didn't take his eyes off it, he would know when the gun was being pulled. At this moment, k.t. told the woman "the very instant … your fiancé sees that right hand begin to move again, he must react swiftly! He must drop to the floor! Just drop! Don't worry about getting hurt. Right hand moves toward inside pocket? Dive! Dive! Dive!" K.t. repeated her instructions like a mantra, making sure the woman understood that the young man must not follow his instinct to turn and run, but must fall to the ground to avoid the bullet.

Understandably, the young woman was extremely distressed. She took the tape with her, promising she would make her fiancé listen. "I will never forget the heartbreaking sensation I experienced as I said goodbye to her that day," says k.t. "This lovely young woman had come specifically to hear about her future marriage. Instead the conversation had been focused on a crime that could not be prevented."

About three weeks after the reading, k.t. received a call from a Miami police officer and later from the young man himself. He had found himself in the exact situation described by k.t., but instead of fleeing he dived to the floor. The bullet from the .357-Magnum only grazed the side of his face. His money (college tuition fees) was safely tucked in his sock.

LEFT: A potentially fatal shooting was narrowly averted through k.t.'s psychic vision of the incident, prior to the event.

ABOVE: Chris Robinson's dream involving IRA terrorists may well have helped police foil an attack on Britain's top-security spy base, GCHQ, in Cheltenham.

Like most of the other psychics who perceive "clues" with their sixth sense, Robinson's take a bit of interpretation, but his own analysis of his dreams has become more accurate. He has demonstrated his abilities on television, with considerable success. More often than not, objects are placed in a sealed box and Chris is asked to dream about the contents the night before the show. He always takes the pages of his dream diary with him, which he says proves the information has come from his dreams, and has baffled more than one presenter with his strange, but seemingly true, dream powers.

An article published in an issue of *Focus* magazine in September 1997,

RIGHT: Robinson believes his "specialty" is crimes involving terrorism, because he has learnt to recognize the associated signs in his dreams.

Backed by the Best

One of the earliest psychic detectives to receive endorsement from the police was Kansas-born Gene Dennis, whose mother, according to Lyons and Truzzi, claimed her daughter's promotional trip to the west coast of the United States in 1922, instigated 800,000 letters requesting help and a three-year movie deal when she was only sixteen. Dennis was tested by the police in New York City when she was seventeen and again she allegedly amazed her audience, giving a constant stream of information on cases they were having difficulties with. In her first year appearing as a clairvoyant on the vaudeville circuit in 1921, the young Dennis was able to charge $2,500 a performance!

Dennis's most outstanding claim to fame was that in March 1924, a mother sued her for giving false information about her son and thereby obtaining money by fortune-telling. The case went to court and Dennis appeared with some highly respectable character witnesses, not only was a police captain from the Department of Missing Persons Bureau present to give evidence on her behalf, but Harry Houdini (above), the infamous magician, and well-known skeptic, turned up in court for Dennis.

ABOVE: Detective Chief Superintendent Eric Rundle headed the Tate case – the first in Britain to have police approval for the involvement of psychic detectives.

LEFT: Andrew Wilson (center) heads a special paranormal research unit, brought in to investigate the disappearance of Genette Tate.

describes how Robinson got the police to take him seriously: "Robinson dreamt that Irish terrorists were plotting a bombing campaign from a Cheltenham [England] hotel. He told a police friend about it. When it comes to terrorism the police welcome any leads they can get so they decided to check it out. A few days later, five IRA members were arrested in a hotel in Cheltenham."

Cracking the cases

Another British psychic detective is Robert Cracknell. Although not so much in the public eye as he was, Cracknell has worked on crime cases if not in conjunction with, then with the blessing of, certain British police forces. Cracknell and distinguished author Colin Wilson were invited to Aylesbeare police search headquarters in Devon after the strange disappearance of Genette Tate, a thirteen-year-old Devon schoolgirl. The young girl was reported missing after her paper round, only minutes after passing two of her friends. It was Saturday, August 19, 1978.

Colin Wilson recounts, in his book *The Psychic Detectives*, that he had just been made aware of Cracknell's supposed abilities through a mutual acquaintance. He asked if Cracknell would try to help find the girl. The psychic agreed, and although he hadn't heard anything about the investigation, he made a series of predictions on a television program, which so impressed the police officer in charge of the case, that Cracknell was called in.

The Schilling Murder

ABOVE: Nancy Myer, who claims an eighty to ninety percent success rate in the hundreds of cases she has worked on.

In July 1979, the Anne Arundel County Police Department sent Detective Jim Moore and another officer to an office in Newark, Delaware. The office was the base for Nancy Myer, now one of the most respected psychic detectives working in the United States. The two police officers were baffled by a case involving the brutal murder of Leonetta Schilling from Pasadena, Maryland, whose husband had come home for lunch and found her dying of stab wounds, the result of a horrific attack. The woman had been on the telephone to her daughter less than an hour before her husband had found her, and no witnesses came forward. The police were at a dead end.

When Detective Moore visited Myer, he was initially skeptical, but took along photos of the crime scene after Leonetta had been taken to hospital, a photo of the victim taken close to the time of her death, and a map of the area. They also brought a "file folder full of mug shots," according to Myer. "Basically it was a file of everyone who had ever stabbed anyone in that area, or been caught with a knife, they told me. At that time in the investigation, they had no idea where to turn."

Looking over the photographs, Myer recalls "a modest, well-kept home. The morning's dishes were in the drainer, with the dishrag spread out to dry. The poignancy of those images has stayed with me always. It looked like any ordinary house, with no visual clue at all to the horrible violence that had occurred there."

From simply looking at the photos of the house, Myer was able to go into specific details about what had happened in those frightening final few minutes. She says the photos were "chock full of information," and describes how she thinks that photos store information and that for some reason she is able to "tap into that store of information and decipher it. Once I set that ability in motion it's like looking at a movie screen in my head."

"It is difficult sometimes to understand exactly what I am seeing, as the audio movie is not very good. Visually it is excellent, but the sound is not good. I also get it in spurts. Short scenes, as if someone has edited it. Each scene, however, will carry an awesome amount of information. My test is to figure out what I am looking at, describe it as precisely as I can without editorializing at all … Just telling it as I am seeing it."

Myer told the police exactly what she saw in her vision while she was looking at the Schilling photos. She said that the victim knew her attacker well and that she had an almost mother–son relationship with him, although he wasn't her son. She had known her attacker since his birth and even babysat for him. Myer says the images she received were distressing to say the least. "The brutality and overkill of the assault was shocking to me. He had once loved her. I could not understand the hatred that now poured out of

"The arrest occurred one week after the police were in my office on July 6 or 7. The case they put together using my information was so solid it has stood the tests of all the appeals courts."

him into this murderous attack. Shocked, she could only plead for her life, she was no match for his youth and insane strength."

Myer managed to give the police a full physical description of the assailant and surprised officers with the information that there had actually been two witnesses to the crime. One, a young man, had driven to the Schilling house with the attacker. She was able to give them a full physical description of this accomplice and the vehicle that the two men had traveled in. "I pointed to a street on the map," she recalls, "and began to describe the vehicle and the accomplice driving it. It had been parked on a side street near the victim's house. The vehicle was facing the victim's front door. The driver could not have helped seeing the killer leave the house covered in blood.

"I also pointed to the area across the street from the victim's house. There had been another witness to the killer leaving Leonetta's house. The witness also knew the killer and had seen him covered in blood. She was afraid to come forward."

RIGHT: On the Rosenbloom case, Myer learns to rappel to help locate the missing body.

BELOW: Being interviewed by TV crews helps record Myer's input on a case.

The police apparently left the office raring to go. From Myer's description of the assailant, police believed the attacker was the victim's nephew, but were eager to trace these two apparent witnesses. Following Myer's information, they pulled in the accomplice for questioning. He was so shaken by the amount the police seemed to know, that he turned state's evidence against the killer. "One week after my reading," says Myer, "Leonetta's nephew, Allen Glenn Finke, was arrested and charged with the June 8, 1979, murder of Mrs. Leonetta Schilling."

The witness from across the road fled after police questioning, confirming Myer's information, and the accomplice was charged with being an accessory after the fact, as he had not known Finke was going to commit murder. Finke is still serving his sentence.

ABOVE: *A trailer park similar to the scene where Candace Augustus and her son were found dead. Police relied on psychic Bill Ward to help them track down the killer.*

Wilson describes how Chief Inspector Don Crabb, who was involved with the Tate case, personally showed Cracknell the girl's bicycle, the area where she disappeared, and even took him to meet the girl's parents. Cracknell got some strong images about the case: That Genette had been knocked from her bike and dragged over a hedge by a man intent on raping her, but the rape didn't take place. According to Wilson, Cracknell felt "the man was a laboring type, with a record of mental illness." Despite all of Cracknell's feelings about the case (he receives images without having to employ the techniques used by other psychics, such as psychometry), he didn't help locate the body or the supposed killer. Genette Tate has never been found—she simply disappeared into thin air.

Although Cracknell was never proved right or wrong, because the case was never solved, Wilson was impressed enough by the psychic detective to help him find a publisher for his autobiography, and wrote "if the Genette Tate investigation raised doubts in my mind about Bob's powers, his performance in the case of the Yorkshire Ripper allayed them ... Cracknell spent some time in Yorkshire, at the invitation of the police and of a Sunday newspaper, wandering around the murder sites." According to Wilson, Cracknell made some pretty accurate predictions, which were recorded by newspapers such as the respected *Yorkshire Post*.

Not only did he correctly pinpoint the area where Peter Sutcliffe lived, Cracknell's prediction of the date of the Ripper's last attack was only a few days out. His description of the house the Sutcliffes lived in was also surprisingly accurate.

A proven track record

Another publicity-shy psychic detective is the Illinois-based Bill Ward who allegedly realized he was psychic after going through the trauma of the Vietnam War as an army medic. Ward doesn't like being tested and only works with police departments who seek his help.

He is quite unusual in that he not only uses psychometry on his cases, but helps with personality profiles by using astrology, auras, and biorhythms. He is said to be able to practice psychokinesis (moving objects with the power of his mind), and is also interested in hypnosis. Stories about him in the press describe him as being seventy-five to eighty percent accurate with his predictions, and he alleges to have worked with police on more than 400 homicide cases.

Jim Lippard, writing in *Psychic Sleuths*, describes the 1987 Illinois case of Candace Augustus and her eleven-year-old son, who were both found dead in their trailer-park home. Robert Fair, a man who also lived at the park, had disappeared and he was the police's chief suspect. The police at Dixmoor called Bill Ward (he is well known by the local police and has been used in multiple local cases), to see if he could shed any light on what had happened and where the suspect had gone.

Ward predicted that the suspect had taken the woman's car and had headed off toward his mother's house, but he had dumped the car half way there and continued on public transport. The suspect actually gave himself up, but Ward had already told the police what to expect from the confession, and had even allegedly used personality profiling through working out the suspect's biorhythms, to inform the detectives how best to carry out the interrogation. According to Lippard, Ward was presented with a certificate which thanked him for his "invaluable information" and "psychic rendition of the crime and psychological profile of the offender."

Judy Belle is a self-taught American psychic who says she is terrible at locating anything, but seems to have a good success rate at having visions that recreate the scene of the crime. In this way she can see who was there, whether there were eyewitnesses, what type of vehicles were around, and so on, and snippets like that often help the police with their investigations. Although it didn't result in an arrest, Belle "saw" the suspect's car at the scene of a double murder, which was later confirmed by an independent witness. The witness didn't see the suspect, though, and regrettably the police could not prosecute on the basis of psychic evidence only.

ABOVE: Psychics have found new ways to utilize their detection skills. Stephan Schwartz has successfully used remote viewing techniques to excavate archaeological sites.

Alan Vaughan, American psychic, author, and honorary doctor of parapsychology, worked with a group set up in 1977 by Stephan Schwartz, a former U.S. naval intelligence officer. The Los Angeles Mobius Group, as the organization was known, consisted of psychics who could be called upon for research purposes into the uses of psychic ability. They didn't necessarily specialize in crime detection, but more than once found themselves working on cases, helping out the conventional detectives.

Vaughan says he was asked to assist the group on a missing girl case in 1981. It was the first time he had used his abilities to work with the police, but according to Vaughan, his psychic information was extremely accurate. When he was handed a photograph of the girl, he psychometrized that she was dead, that she had been murdered, and that her murderer had been some kind of teacher. When the police tracked down the killer, he was, in fact, the girl's karate teacher. Vaughan told *Fate* magazine that the district attorney involved with the case, Mick Ranck, has since appeared on television and given Vaughan's psychic information an eighty-five percent accuracy rating.

Vaughan, like many psychic detectives, teaches his "intuitive techniques" as a way to earn money, because for the psi sleuth, solving crimes rarely pays. Despite these working detectives having the backing of often more than one police department, most feel awkward about profiting from other people's misery. Writing books, making TV appearances, charging for interviews, and so on, are really the only legitimate ways they can make money from their special talent without the skeptics accusing them of being mercenary.

CHAPTER FOUR

Government and Psychic Sleuths

The Secret World of Psi Spies

The world of secret agents and psychically advanced mind games played across cold war divides seems to be within the realms of James Bond-style fiction, or perhaps more aptly, X Files' conspiracy theory. Within the constraints of our normal understanding, the idea that governments would be spending time and money on training a group of "psychics" is, as one official spokesperson put it, "laughable." However, as is often the case when researching the boundaries of our accepted ideologies, fact is stranger than fiction, and both the United States government and the former USSR government have published details of research they carried out into the potential of psychic mindpower.

The U.S. government has admitted investigating the possibilities of psi during the 1960s and 1970s in programs estimated to have cost approximately $20 million. The Central Intelligence Agency (CIA) actually had a parapsychology department that tested such well-known paranormal personalities as Uri Geller in the hope that those with clairvoyant abilities could enlighten researchers as to how the psychically receptive mind worked. American programs into psi and remote viewing—the ability to "see" events at distant locations—were direct responses to reports from Russia that their psychic warfare program was advanced beyond anything the West could imagine. Even the usually covert Russian government has made files public since the 1950s, which expose various laboratories throughout the former Soviet Union whose sole purpose was research into the power of the human mind and its potential in areas such as spying, remote control, and remote influencing.

What is even more intriguing is that these are just the facts that these superpowers have admitted. If the KGB and the CIA have been publicly linked to psychic programs in the 1960s and 1970s, what is going on behind closed doors now? Allegedly, some of the brightest minds are now exploring the boundaries of psychic ability. Despite repeated denials that research is still taking place, it is not unreasonable, considering past track records, to believe certain governments are funding the development of a totally new kind of weapon—a superpowerful psychic detective, who not only can access a different reality, but can use it to control, maim, and even kill.

One of the most astonishing things to have come out of the cold war was the realization that both the United States and the former Soviet Union had been meddling in what some people still thought of as the occult. The shadowy and not-yet-understood world of psychic ability was being studied by some of the highest ranking scientific minds in the world ... and it probably still is.

Psychic research is a very secretive area, not least because there are so many skeptics, and it requires substantial funding for it to be investigated properly. The lure of the ultimate weapons system, however, has to be the most tempting prospect for any government, particularly those who are involved in a complex fight of ideologies. If one side is able to develop the power of the mind to the point where objects and people could be "remote influenced," then enemy weaponry could be sabotaged and potentially heads of state might be influenced in their decision making. The whereabouts of submarines, army headquarters, nuclear development establishments, and so on, could all be located and mapped by a psychic spy sitting thousands of miles away in an office. Can this extraordinary unseen force be shaped, harnessed, and refined to the point where negative energies can force individuals to act in a certain way? Would the highly trained psychic spy one day be able to commit remote murder?

The lack of information on the subject made the idea of world superpowers investigating psychics, mediums, and hypnotists either laughable or the stuff that science fiction and James Bond were made of. Conspiracy theorists reveled in the idea of a government-funded team of clairvoyants psychically trying to bring down the entire U.S. infrastructure ... then, in

RIGHT: Would everyone's favorite spy, James Bond, be made redundant by the new psychic operative?

BELOW: The CIA headquarters in Washington, D.C., which funded U.S. psychic spy programs.

1995, an astonishing document came to light, which caused sensational media reports.

CIA admit to psychic spies

On September 6, 1995, the CIA released a statement saying it was "reviewing available information and past research programs concerning parapsychological phenomena, mainly 'remote viewing,' to determine whether they might have any utility for intelligence collection." This sounded innocuous enough but for those in the know, the CIA had been looking into the possibilities of remote viewing for decades.

Media interest soared. After all, although they countered with the phrase that it proved "unpromising," the CIA press release finally stated in black and white that "the CIA sponsored research on this subject in the 1970s." It also said the history of such controversial research was in the process of being declassified.

That wasn't the first the public had heard of the U.S. government being linked with parapsychology. Former president Jimmy Carter had alluded to the use of remote viewing in helping locate a downed spy plane during his term in office, and there were several

BELOW: Ex-president Jimmy Carter has admitted the CIA investigated the usefulness of ESP and remote viewing during the 1970s while he was in office.

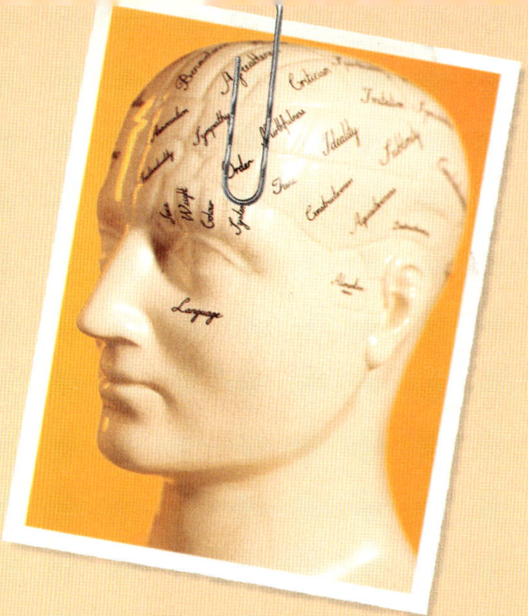

Remote Viewing: The Psychic Skill

Descriptions of the technicalities of remote viewing become very complicated, and vary from practitioner to practitioner. Some believe it is a truly paranormal state where the viewer enters an alternative reality, while others believe it can be explained in more scientific terms, and describe it as simply being more in tune with a sixth sense that occurs in all of us.

The multitude of courses running, especially in the U.S., purporting to be able to teach anyone to tap into this exciting new skill, suggests that anyone with an interest in the area has the potential to become a remote viewer.

Remote viewing is often thought of as taking place between two people, one being the "sender" of an image and the other being a "receiver," as in the famous British television demonstration on The Paranormal World of Paul McKenna when TV presenter Shaw Taylor was the sender of an impression of where he was standing and Joe McMoneagle, one of Project Stargate's psychic spies, successfully received his images. There are other forms the phenomenon takes though, where an individual can allegedly receive images and sounds of places or events, either in the present, past, or the future. Those working with controlled remote viewing (CRV), the methods used and developed by Ingo Swann, concentrate on what they call "real-world" targets; although they don't tend to use the method to glean information about the past, instead they deal with questions of the here and now.

Lyn Buchanan is Executive Director of P>S>I (Problems>Solutions>Innovations), a Maryland company that offers controlled-remote-viewing services and training, and hosts the CRV homepage on the Internet. Buchanan's website (http://www.crviewer.com/) contains excellent information about the history, background, and practical applications of remote viewing, along with the layman's description: "Put most simply, CRV is a highly structured methodology which allows a person to set up a path between his/her conscious and subconscious minds for the purpose of passing questions one way and answers the other, without the fear of pollution along the way."

"whistle-blowers" who had spoken to the media about such projects as Stargate, Grill Flame, Sun Streak, and Scanate—but the 1995 statement fired a lot of follow-up research.

Where the psi-trained mind can go

Angela Thompson Smith is a British-born, American-based remote viewer who has worked on projects "ranging from stolen art works, the Unabomber case, archaeological sites, missing persons, historical enigmas, space exploration, Earth changes and future technologies." She is also the author of *Remote Perceptions: Out-of-Body Experiences, Remote Viewing, and Other Normal Abilities*, an examination of remote viewing with a foreword written by the father of the subject, Ingo Swann.

In the book she explains how anyone can remote view with training, and goes on to list the practical implications (aside from spying for the CIA, of course!). Thompson Smith writes, "In the future, remote viewing could be used to locate astronauts lost in space, to seek out lost or nonfunctioning satellites, and report on space emergencies. The mind is able to go where machines or the physical body cannot go. An adept viewer could enter a hostile environment, encountering flood, fire, chemicals, or other substances. A remote viewer could go out into space, into the hub of a nuclear reactor after a melt-down; the possibilities are endless."

The implications for governments and the individuals who could potentially harness this power are theoretically huge, but the idea that the CIA had actually funded research into something so "paranormal," gave society the impression those in power believed there was something in it. It would be ironic if police forces were rejecting help from psychics who believed they had somehow remote viewed or sensed a murder, while the central government was paying the wages of people who professed to have the exact same abilities.

The U.S. research came about because of the threat of psychic warfare from the former Soviet Union. The Russians had been interested in the potential uses of psi powers before; *The Washington Post* (August 7, 1977) reported that parapsychologist Dr. Andrija Puharich had given a lecture to the Defense Department in 1952 called "On the Possible Usefulness of Extrasensory Perception in Psychological Warfare." By 1969, U.S. intelligence services were aware money was being poured into research by the Russians, but rumor and disinformation were rife.

The use of psychic spies by world leaders isn't new—one only has to think about such shadowy figures as the Russian mystic Rasputin and Adolf Hitler's supposed obsession with the world of the occult. Although Hitler's personal interest in areas of the paranormal has probably been exaggerated, there are numerous stories of high-ranking Nazis consulting psychics and astrologers. Heinrich Himmler, for example, seems to have been obsessed with the search for the answers to harnessing psychic power, and even supposedly ordered a mission to hunt for the mythical Holy Grail.

What is known, is that despite openly persecuting many psychics, the Nazi party commissioned research into dowsing and other psychic abilities in 1939. They were also famously tricked into thinking that the British were successfully employing the services of a psychic dowser to locate German submarines, which is why they had the edge over the Germans. It led to the Nazis employing psychics of their own who pored over maps making various predictions and ultimately helped the Germans lose the war.

Even today, research into parapsychology is much more accepted in Eastern Europe, with Russia, Czechoslovakia, and Bulgaria all having state-funded

ABOVE: The former KGB headquarters in Moscow, Russia. The feared state security police were no doubt the source of much disinformation about the Soviet psychic research program.

BELOW: Red Square in Moscow, a one-time symbol of the cold war, which generated so much paranoia and distrust—the perfect climate for espionage to flourish.

Psychic Spying: A Corporate Winner?

Paranormal Management Systems (PMS) was the first British-based consultancy company to "take up the gauntlet thrown down by the CIA," and take the study of remote viewing into the realms of the private sector. Based in Brighton, England, Tim Rifat, the company director, has been researching and practicing the practical uses of remote viewing for more than ten years. Now the company offers courses to businesses and private individuals who want to harness the advantage of possessing a sixth sense.

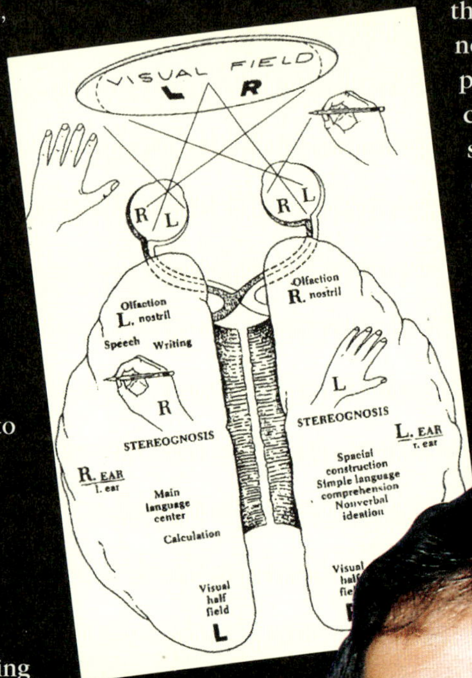

Although MI6, the British intelligence agency, are rumored to have shown some interest in the idea of psychic spying, Britain hasn't been at the forefront of government-sponsored parapsychological research, and for the majority of the general public, remote viewing is something new. Despite this, interest in PMS has been impressive.

Advertising its product as providing "a scientific overview of paranormal and psychological techniques suitable for organizations that need to maintain their competitive edge," Rifat's training courses promise to give the individual an insight into their competitors' plans, ideas, and even thought patterns. Although it sounds a bit sinister, Rifat's emphasis is on a positive application of the powers. Indeed, the personal course concentrates quite heavily on using the technique of remote influencing primarily for therapeutic healing purposes.

PMS has done extensive research into brain states and how our perception of the world works. We currently define our reality in terms of our five senses, but, as Rifat says, this is limiting. His teaching methods enable people to tap into a different branch of themselves, which then allows more information about our reality through to our consciousness. There is nothing supernatural about the process; remote viewing could be compared to taking blinkers off, so suddenly a much wider picture comes into view.

Most of the British course is based on simple relaxation and stress management techniques, which are the key to focusing the mind and

LEFT: PMS's literature explains how to control your own brainwave activity.

BELOW: Tim Rifat, leading British proponent of remote viewing.

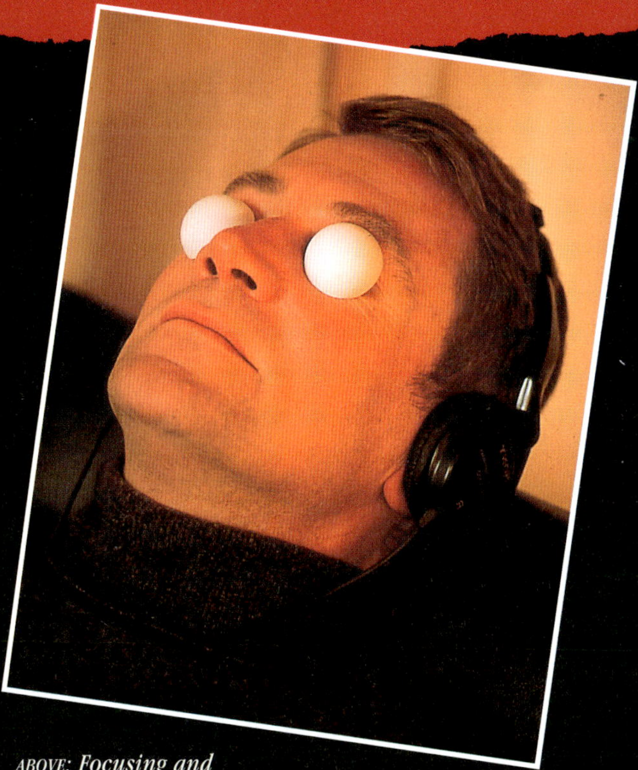

ABOVE: Focusing and clearing the mind of outside influences, such as sound and vision, is the key to successful remote viewing.

preparing it to be receptive to the idea of remote viewing. Once free from the usual clutter that clogs up our brains, and when both the body and mind are in a calm state, there is enough energy to access the brain state that allows an individual to experience things beyond our usual understanding of reality. PMS is simply suggesting we can trigger a state in ourselves that scientists have already proved can be triggered by machines, such as the Ganzfeld device, which is used to dull the senses such as sight and hearing, while applying small electromagnetic waves to the brain, inducing altered consciousness. Much of PMS's interest lies with the potential such an untapped source of knowledge could have for businesses. Not only can remote viewing allow an extraordinary insight into a competitor's activities, it has an untapped potential for management-staff relations. PMS advertises "instruction in remote viewing, remote sensing and remote influencing—providing techniques that allow leaks in organizations to be found—personal evaluation and persons important to one's aims to be influenced—all at a distance." For the business tycoon with a paranoid streak, PMS could be the ultimate answer—but initiation into the arts of the psychic sixth sense has its price—and it isn't cheap!

Psychic Healing

Tim Rifat's research into remote viewing, and more specifically, the "biological field effects" around our brains that are responsible for this latent psychic ability, has opened up areas which are even more hard to comprehend than psychic spying. The PMS research allegedly has the potential not only to help cure major diseases such as cancer, but may also be able to extend human lifetime. Research is in the early stages, but "PMS is developing a promising paranormal psychoneuroimmunological approach to the amplification of the immune system." Much of this area is shrouded in jargon, but what, in essence, Rifat believes is that the power of remote-influencing another individual doesn't necessarily have to be for negative reasons, as world governments initially planned with the use of psychic spying. While rumors have circulated that the Soviets tried bombarding American human targets with electronically manufactured microwaves, the same pulses may well be produced naturally by our brains.

If the brain has the potential to negatively affect another human being's brain state, then it follows the reverse would be true as well. PMS believes utilizing the same techniques that teach the individual to remote view and then applying them to your own body can have a highly beneficial effect on the immune system. The company cites the work of Dr. Carl Simonton, who describes himself as a pioneer in psychoneuroimmunology, and is Founder and Medical Director of the Simonton Cancer Center in California, where he trained "terminal cancer patients to visualize their white blood cells eating up their cancerous tissue." Simonton says his methods can demonstrate "an increase in survival time and improvement in quality of life." Can the power of the psychically trained mind hold the potential to cure our own bodies? Rifat thinks so.

research institutes investigating the practical uses of psi. This could be because of their long history of seers, prophets, and mystics, or it could be because they know something those in the West don't.

According to the little information that has filtered out to the West, Eastern Europe has always been way ahead in the race to explore extrasensory perception (ESP). Serious research, funded by the government, into paranormal phenomena has been conducted since the early 1950s, possibly even earlier. The Soviets refer to "bioenergetic research" instead of "parapsychology," but regardless of the terminology, they, too, are looking for ways to prove a "sixth sense" exists, and that it is a harnessable commodity that can be used for military intelligence purposes.

Soviet sensory perception

Far from being reticent about the idea of funding for such programs, scientists were instructed to actively seek out people professing to possess psychic or clairvoyant talents, and then test them. Laboratories were set up all over the former USSR, and until the cold war, the Russians were relatively open about their new discipline of science. Then suddenly its potential was deemed top secret and the world of the Russian scientists was plunged into darkness and overseen by the KGB.

One of the few authoritative sources on paranormal developments in Eastern Europe is *Psychic Discoveries: Behind the Iron Curtain*, and its follow-up *Psychic Discoveries: The Iron Curtain Lifted*, by Sheila Ostrander and Lynn Schroeder, two American writers and researchers specializing in the paranormal. Their first book caused a storm when it was published in 1971. It was really the first the American public had heard about "psychic warfare," but it wasn't the first the U.S. government had heard. It did, however, backup the intelligence reports of huge amounts of Soviet money being poured into this research. (According to remote-viewing expert Ingo Swann, a man central to psychic spy-ring research, by "1970 it was discovered that the Soviets were spending approximately 60 million rubles per year ... and over 300 million by 1975" on psychic research.) The book also provided what seemed like incredible proof that the Soviets were getting results.

Ostrander and Schroeder report that the former KGB Major General Oleg Kalugin is on record saying "Russian scientists have been very successful in developing psychic warfare devices." Kalugin has also told the West that Russian scientists were able to build generators that replicated the psychic force their subjects could emit. Ostrander and Schroeder write, "Kalugin revealed in 1990 that it was Yuri Andropov, head of the KGB from 1967 to 1982 (and later, premier of the USSR), who issued personal orders to push full steam ahead with psychic warfare. Andropov's directive also urged scientists to forget being squeamish about injuring or killing research subjects in the race to achieve their goal."

The psychic generators

Edward Naumov is one of, if not the leading parapsychologist in Russia, who was once arrested and spent a year in labor camps. He is reported in the Ostrander and Schroeder follow-up book, *Psychic Discoveries: The Iron Curtain Lifted*, as saying, "A psychotronic generator can influence an individual or a whole crowd

TOP: Oleg Kalugin, former KGB general, publicly stated that Russian research into ESP had been "very successful."

ABOVE: Yuri Andropov, in his capacity as head of the KGB, pushed research into psychic warfare to new boundaries.

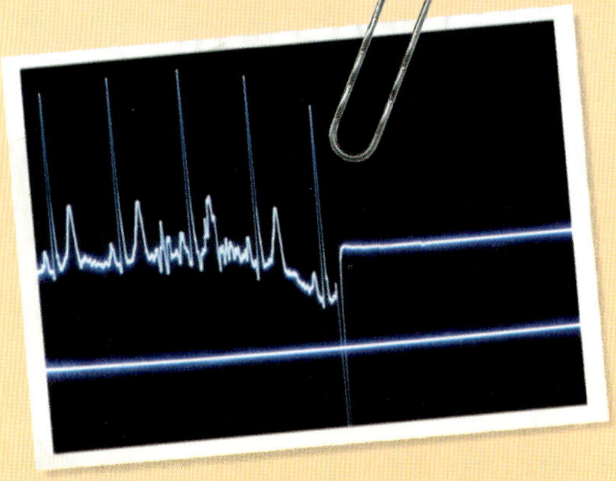

Heart-stopping Stuff

One of the most extraordinary public displays of Eastern European psi power was broadcast on British television during an episode of The Paranormal World of Paul McKenna. The implications of the event, if they were genuine, are huge. Albert Ignatenko, from the Ukraine, claimed he could raise or lower another person's heartbeat or pulse from a distance, without touching them. This was monitored by the production team and, after a period of intense concentration, Ignatenko successfully demonstrated he could remote influence selected individuals.

The implications of this experiment were not explored fully. Critical questions such as whether Ignatenko could slow a heartbeat to the point of death, and why his powers had been honed in such a risky and potentially lethal manner, were not asked. But for all intents and purposes, the program showed a man capable of affecting the health and emotional state of strangers. How comfortable should we be with this information?

of people. It can affect a person's psyche mentally and emotionally. It can affect memory and attention span. A psychotronic device can cause physical fatigue, disorientation, and alter a person's behavior." All this from a device which the Russians supposedly developed by replicating the effects of remote viewers, psychics, dowsers, and telepathists. Naumov told an American TV network he knew "over half a billion rubles were spent on developing psychotronic equipment."

Naumov's talk of psychic generators is perhaps hard to accept, but it worried the U.S. government enough to fund the aforementioned Project Stargate. One of the most interesting stories to come out of this web of psychic intrigue was that the Russians allegedly bombarded the U.S. embassy in Moscow with radiation waves. *The Washington Times* reported on November 15, 1992, that according to U.S. officials, the Russian government was still continuing this psychic "attack" on the embassy. Throughout the 1970s the building was supposed to be the target of a Russian psychotronic experiment, and according to some accounts it was a success. The top floors of the

BELOW: The U.S. embassy in Moscow, which is thought to have been the target of experimental psychotronic radiation waves perpetrated by the Soviets since the 1970s.

ABOVE: The Branch Davidian compound in Waco, Texas, explodes at the end of a 51-day stand-off in 1993.

RIGHT: Did the FBI use Soviet psychic techniques, known as microwave weapons, to try to influence cult leader David Koresh and his loyal followers?

building were eventually protected with reflective materials, but not until after *The Boston Globe* newspaper had reported in 1976 that Ambassador Walter Stoessel had developed a rare blood disease and that two of his predecessors at the embassy had curiously died of cancers.

In an unusual East-West collaboration on psychic-warfare techniques, Ostrander and Schroeder claim the Pentagon invited a team of Russian scientists to America during the 1993 siege in Waco, Texas, where David Koresh and his Branch Davidian followers were holding out against an armed Alcohol, Tobacco and Firearms (ATF) unit of the FBI. While the world watched the stand-off live on its TV screens, the Soviet scientists were allegedly demonstrating the use of psychotronic devices to potentially plant thoughts and feelings in the minds of the cult members. Whether the techniques were used or not isn't known.

According to an article by Owen Mathews, published in *The Moscow Times* on July 11, 1995, and reprinted on the website Citizens Against Human Rights Abuse (http://www.calweb.com/~welsh/index.htm), a civil liberties organization in Russia called the Ecology and Living Environment group, has filed damages against the Russian Federal Security Service (the successor to the KGB secret police) and the Russian government on behalf of "victims of psychotronic experiments." Mathews reported that journalist Yury Vorobyovsky, who has been researching the use of psychotronic weapons, said "The techniques, which include debilitating high-frequency radio waves, hypnotic computer-scrambled sounds, and mind-bending electromagnetic fields, as well as an ultrasound gun capable of killing a cat at fifty meters, were originally developed for medical purposes and adapted into weapons."

Mathews cited the examples given by the president of the pressure group when she said the government was beaming "rays" into her apartment, which meant she wore a helmet to bed to protect herself. While Mathews acknowledges this sounds somewhat far-fetched, the rest of the article looks at the very real problem that since the break up of the USSR and the resulting internal turmoil, the psychotronic weapons, if they exist, are in danger of falling into the wrong hands, most probably those of the Russian Mafia.

Russia isn't the only country accused of testing its psychic weapons on its own citizens. There are numerous conspiracy pages on the Internet, giving censorship-free space to people claiming they have been the victims of government-backed mind control. It is not as improbable as it sounds and, although it does move on from the realms of psychical research, the subject of this book, the CIA has been linked to memory-erasing and brainwashing experiments.

Much of the mind-control research has been developed from studying talented psychics. There seems to be increasing evidence that much of what we refer to as ESP is a naturally occurring system of electromagnetic waves we emit. One Russian scientist believes he may be able to build a machine, according to Ostrander and Schroeder, that specifically replicates the powers of the psychic detective.

Psychometry solved?

Dr. Genady Sergeyev spent considerable time studying Nina Kulagina, one of Russia's most noted psychics. Kulagina's specialty was being able to move objects or levitate them simply using the power of her mind, known as psychokinesis. She was tested repeatedly over a period of thirty years by numerous scientists, and the consistency of her talent was amazing. Dr. Sergeyev measured the fields of energy emanating from the psychic when she was concentrating on her target. His work led him to the conclusion that objects absorb our energies, to the point where it should be possible to read an object and decode whether it has absorbed good, bad, happy, or distressful energy. According to the two American authors, "His sensors work best on 'mute witnesses'—objects or vegetation in the vicinity of violence. Blasts of violent emotions like rage or fear are easiest to decode."

This research would seem to replicate those psychics who work by using psychometry, and who generally claim their talent works best when they know

ABOVE: A scene from the 1962 film The Manchurian Candidate, *which shows a group of U.S. soldiers brainwashed so they can be remotely triggered to kill specific targets.*

BELOW: Nina Kulagina, the Russian psychic star who amazed all who tested her psychokinetic powers, and convinced Dr. Sergeyev that objects could absorb "psychic" energy.

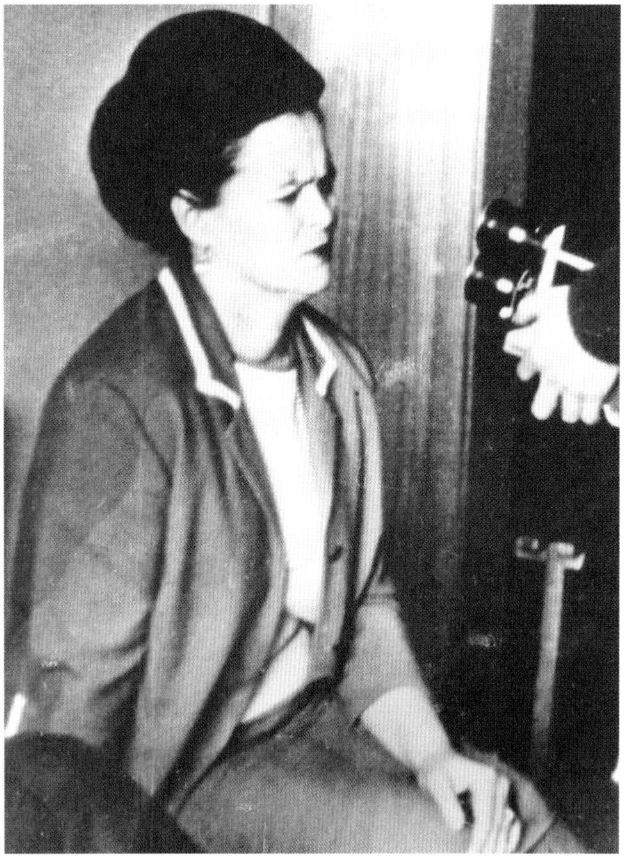

very little about a person or crime, but get the clearest mental images when they are simply handed an object from the crime scene or something personal that belonged to the individual. Are the Russians well on the way to discovering the secrets of the sixth sense? Can they already replicate the talents of our psychic sleuths?

Critics of the West's research, or at least what we know about the West's research, say that it has been dogged by the cynicism of skeptics who have created an atmosphere where someone has to prove emphatically, in terms of our current understanding of science, that ESP exists. Until then, research into its possibilities will always be stunted.

The 1995 public statement by the CIA was part of a general move in America toward more openness and greater freedom of information. As promised, certain declassifed documents alluded to psychic spying programs, the most interesting of which confirmed that for more than two decades the U.S. government, initially via the CIA, had funded organized research into whether psi phenomena like remote viewing "might have any utility for intelligence collection."

BELOW: U.S. psychic Peter Nelson performs a psychometric experiment in an attempt to receive information from the object he is holding.

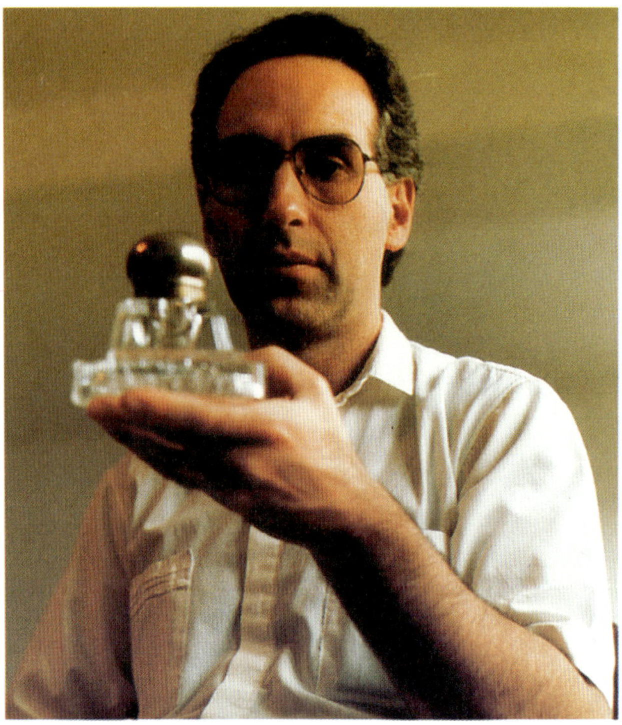

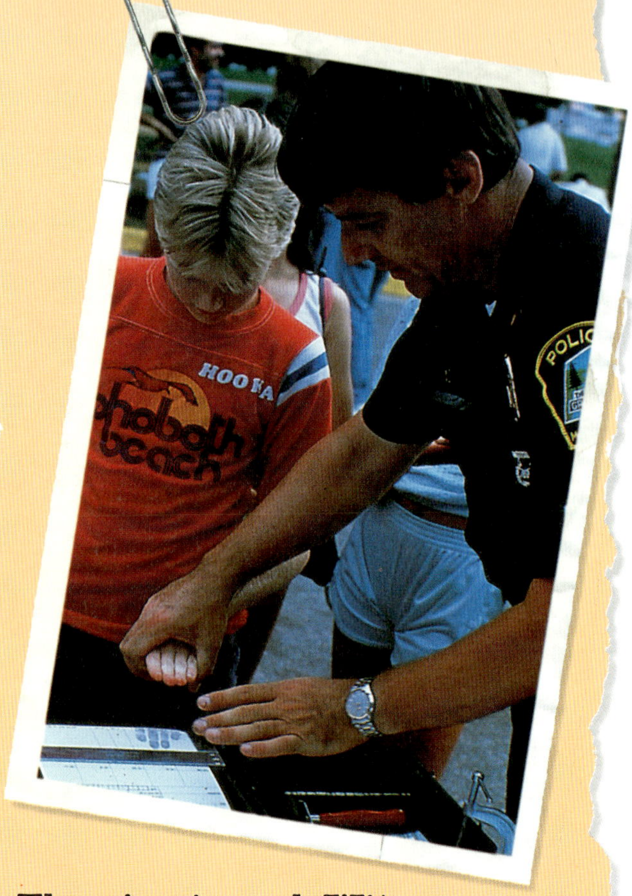

The Assigned Witness Program

Some graduates of the U.S. military remote-viewing programs have found more positive uses for their skills. Former Fort Meade trainee, Lyn Buchanan, now runs the Assigned Witness Program (AWP) through his company P>S>I. AWP is a free public service offering the skills of what are actually psychic detectives, but he calls students of controlled remote viewing. They will help locate missing children, or family members, or even bodies.

Although the publicity material says they can only accept a minimal number of cases at present because of the time taken to remote view properly, AWP would like to work on cases full-time, saying "the rewards of finding a lost child are fantastic." The program operates only at the request of the police, so if a family approaches the AWP, it asks them to go through their investigating officers. This is a sensible precaution and avoids the frustration, AWP says, of having "wasted our time and raised the family's hopes needlessly" in instances when the information is turned over to the police who ignore it because it is from a psychic.

Interestingly, AWP maintains the anonymity of police departments who ask for its help, and so far only one has agreed to endorsing the group publicly. Despite this, Buchanan says he asks all the graduates from his advanced controlled-remote-viewing course to use their skills to help find at least five missing children during their first year after graduation.

The release of 270 pages of research notes into the public domain in July 1995 also unveiled some of the key American personnel from—at least part of—their official shroud of secrecy. Project Stargate had become fact. From 1972 until 1995, official funds were made available to research primarily the phenomenon of remote viewing, with the hope that a gifted individual would be able to remote view into specific targets or even receive messages from others far away.

H. E. Puthoff was working at the Stanford Research Institute (SRI), in Palo Alto, California, researching laser technology. He had previously worked as a naval intelligence officer before deciding to concentrate on a research career. In 1972, he was contacted by two men from the CIA regarding research he had carried out with the New York artist Ingo Swann. Swann claimed he could use his mind to perform feats other people couldn't, and Puthoff had been intrigued.

In a report titled "CIA-Initiated Remote Viewing at Stanford Research Institute," published after the 1995 declassification, Puthoff writes he was told "there was concern in the intelligence community about the level of effort in Soviet parapsychology being funded by the Soviet security services; by Western scientific standards the field was considered nonsense by most working scientists. As a result they had been on the lookout for a research laboratory outside of academia that could handle a quiet low-profile classified investigation, and SRI appeared to fit the bill." Puthoff was to become the director of the SRI, the only CIA-funded "psychic" research project, and would remain so until 1985.

Project Stargate

After twenty-four years of psychic research at Palo Alto, the CIA commissioned an independent evaluation of Project Stargate, which was carried out by the American Institutes for Research (AIR).

LEFT: H. E. Puthoff, founder of the U.S. remote-viewing research and acknowledged expert in the field.

BELOW: The innocuous-looking buildings at Fort Meade, where the U.S. military trained remote viewers.

Although the assessment came to the conclusion that some encouraging work had been conducted by the team and their "psychics," ultimately they had not found any significant way the research could help intelligence operations. Cries of "cover-up" greeted the results, yet the U.S. government has publicly withdrawn funding for its parapsychological research projects and decided not to pursue the research any farther. Edwin May, the director of Stargate following Puthoff's departure, was joined by his former colleagues in condemning the AIR recommendation, but for now it looks as though, in the West at least, government-funded research into the value of psychic spies, is not on the agenda.

The Stargate team under Puthoff and his fellow physicist Russell Targ, is thought to have produced some startling results, and has been credited with providing some of the most solid and consistent evidence for psi powers to date. Although most research was geared toward developing a controllable psychic weapon, following the 1995 release of information, rumors that the team worked on hostage situations, international terrorism, and drug trafficking have emerged. It seems the psychic crime-fighters weren't confined to the problems of individuals, but were trying to infiltrate crime syndicates on a global scale.

Stargate concentrated on developing and testing remote viewing. The Stargate team consisted of a small group of remote viewers, most notably: Swann; Pat Price, a retired police commissioner; and Hella Hammid, a photographer. In 1974, the CIA challenged the team to remote view a Soviet site that they wanted more information on. In Puthoff's notes he says this wasn't their most successful experiment, but it is declassified so it can be talked about. Price, who had discovered rings around Jupiter using remote viewing, before space exploration had confirmed this, was the remote viewer charged with the task. Targ, Puthoff's colleague, described Price as "one of the most outstanding remote viewers to walk though the doors of SRI."

The lengthy report, filed at the time by the Stargate team, detailed how "to determine the utility of remote viewing under operational conditions, a long-distance remote viewing experiment was carried out on a sponsor-designated target of current interest, an unidentified research center at Semipalatinsk, USSR." In other words, the CIA was paying the wages of a psychic spy who was supposed to tell them what was going on in a secret base in Russia ... not just the realms of *The X Files*!

Price was an interesting character who not only had close links with the police, but believed wholeheartedly in the power of his own mind. It is thought he worked on the Patty Hearst kidnapping case as well as other crimes, but on a day-to-day level he believed he could influence the weather and things like traffic lights—simply by concentrating. Price, like many of the remote viewers employed at SRI, believed he had remote viewed alien bases, not only on other planets, but on earth as well. The circumstances of Price's death have been called suspicious by some researchers. In July 1975, he was planning to travel back to the institute, after about a year in which he wasn't involved with the trials, when he suddenly died of a heart attack. No autopsy was performed and conspiratorial rumors have circulated suggesting maybe the KGB were nervous about America's most successful psychic spy returning to work. Certainly after Price died, the remote viewing program was scaled down considerably.

TOP: One of the most successful of the SRI remote viewers was Ingo Swann, a former artist from New York City.

BOTTOM: Physicist Russell Targ joined Puthoff to lead Project Stargate, in a quest to test and develop the potential of psi.

ABOVE: *A typical assignment for a Stanford psychic would involve remote-viewing Soviet government buildings or military installations, in order to gather intelligence.*

BELOW: *Uri Geller takes part in a psi experiment conducted by Dr. Elmar Gruber on a European TV show. He now keeps his distance from any potential involvement in psychic spying.*

The world's psychic superstar

The SRI also tested the powers of Israeli psychic Uri Geller. Geller specializes in psychokinesis, and the Russians were conducting many experiments with their own versions of Geller. According to his autobiography, *The Geller Effect*, he was subjected to more than six weeks of intensive tests in 1972. These were just some among the many Geller has undergone during his career, but this time the link with the psychic spying program was obvious. Geller was asked to demonstrate moving various instruments, and, interestingly, was asked to read the mind of a computer, by trying to duplicate what was on a screen, just as he can duplicate what another human has drawn. This he apparently did successfully.

In the same book, Geller also talks about several meetings with a mysterious man called "Mike" who claimed he was part of the CIA. (Although Geller says he never showed any official documentation, Mike was privy to certain knowledge about Geller that wasn't in the public domain.) Mike convinced Geller certain members of the CIA did believe it was worth investigating psychic ability, and that it may be advantageous to them both to work together. It was certainly advantageous for Geller, who was granted unlimited entry to the U.S. on his passport, through connections with his new colleague.

Mike, in return, had a whole "shopping list" of things he wanted to know if Geller could do for the CIA. Concentrating on the Soviet embassy in Mexico, Mike wanted to know if Geller could walk around the outside of the building and provide information, such as where the computers were kept and where various rooms were situated. He also wanted to know if Geller could erase tapes, "see" people who were in the building, and even "read" secret security combinations.

This time, Geller obliged. He walked around the outside of the embassy and jotted down psychic impressions that he received. How successful he was in this exercise, he wasn't told. Later in his career though, Geller realized how sensitive his powers were. He was, again according to his autobiography, asked to try to perform all sorts of seemingly innocent tasks, which later turned out to have military connections. He was asked to telepathically change fellow humans' behavior. "Among my tasks," he wrote, "were to wake people from sleep, to induce dreams into their minds, to implant certain suggestions that would cause them to change their opinions about things, or to make them reveal information." In essence, Geller was being tested to see whether he would be useful as a psychic spy.

Throughout his book, Geller refers to working toward world peace. He abhors the idea of using psychic ability against other countries or people, and has understandably decided to participate in much less research work. However, as they say, actions speak louder than words, and although Geller himself has never gone out of his way to gain publicity from the meeting, it is highly significant to anyone remotely intrigued by the link between psychics and world governments that Geller was invited to Geneva to attend the February 1987 U.S./Soviet disarmament talks. The world's most famous psychic was asked to mingle with some of the world's most important leaders. Whether Geller's bombardment of positive thought power was the catalyst behind Gorbachev's medium-range nuclear disarmament U-turn, has to remain speculation.

ABOVE: No longer just fiction or conspiracy theory, the CIA can now be directly linked to research programs investigating ESP and the military potential of mindpower.

Major David Morehouse

Major David Morehouse, now retired from the U.S. Army, has published an alarming account of his involvement with the U.S. government's psychic spy program. Based in two hutlike buildings in Fort Meade, Morehouse was recruited to work with an already existing team of remote viewers on a project named Sun Streak.

His book, titled Psychic Warrior, details how he was hit on the head with a bullet (it ricocheted off his helmet), while serving in Jordan in 1987. This incident subsequently triggered out-of-body experiences and the awakening of his psychic abilities. This led to his enrollment with the Sun Streak program, where he recounts being used to carry out all types of psychic spying missions. Primarily, Morehouse says he was used to spy on enemy targets, but that it was this aspect of the work that finally convinced him he must stop.

Alleging that he was asked to bombard the Iraqi leader Saddam Hussein with negative mental waves, Morehouse says he finally realized the power to remote view and remote influence should be put to good use not bad, such as healing possibilities. It was at that point, according to his book, that the trouble started. He claims he was harassed by authorities for revealing his intention to tell the public what he knew. The harassment went all the way from phone calls to a potentially lethal gas attack on his family home—allegedly.

The book is full of conspiracy, subterfuge, and cover-up. It closely rivals The X Files for high-paranoia, action-filled drama—yet Morehouse claims it is all true. Others who also worked on the government-funded remote-viewing program, often for substantially longer than Morehouse's 1988–1990 stint, have claimed the Psychic Warrior account is more fiction than fact, aiming more for a Hollywood movie contract than the gallant aim of speaking the truth.

While Morehouse has gained public sympathy (and high book sales), Jim Schnabel, journalist and author of the 1997 book Remote Viewers: The Secret History of America's Psychic Spies, thoroughly investigated the Morehouse story. After talking to many people involved with the program, Schnabel wrote what could be considered an antidote to the book, in an article titled "An American Hero": "to tag every piece of fiction in the Morehouse book would mean commenting on virtually every page."

Muddled fact, muddled fiction

Just how successful all this psychic subterfuge was or is, isn't known. Ingo Swann issued a rebuttal statement on December 1, 1995, in response to the dismissive September release of the CIA-commissioned report into the usefulness of remote viewing. In his statement, Swann goes as far as he can—presumably much of what he knows is still classified information—to justify the $20 million of taxpayers' money spent on the research.

He says it is crucial that the public and media understand the U.S. government didn't decide on a whim to suddenly pour huge amounts of public money into studying psychics and the paranormal, rather that the research was commissioned as a direct result of information coming out of Russia. The whole research program was instigated, according to Swann, as a means of "threat analysis." The United States needed to know how dangerous the Soviet psychotronics research really was.

Saying that, the team working on the threat analysis supposedly made some interesting results. Swann says: "A great deal was learned for those $20 million, and our nation received a lot back for the buck spent. Remote viewers did help find SCUD missiles, did help find secret biological and chemical warfare projects, did locate tunnels and extensive underground facilities, and identify their purposes. Not all of the time, of course, and sometimes imperfectly so."

Although the official CIA-backed report stated that the remote viewers had an accuracy rating of about fifteen percent, Swann says this is the level untrained individuals often achieve. "The minimum accuracy needed by the clients [presumably the various government agencies involved] was sixty-five percent. In the later stages of the development [training] part of the effort, this accuracy level was achieved and often consistently exceeded."

Interestingly, although Swann is understandably disappointed that research has been toned down, he suggests skeptics of the power of remote viewing should "begin by considering psychics who successfully help the police," then follow up with the idea that those who display a little natural psychic ability can be trained to develop it and hone it into a fully developed skill. So the father of remote viewing research believes at least some of the world's psychic detectives are on to something.

BELOW: MI6 headquarters in London, England. The British remain tight-lipped about spying methods, not only during the cold war years, but also today.

CHAPTER FIVE

Foreseeing the Future for Psychic Powers

Unlocking the Potential of the Mind

What can the existence of people who call themselves psychic detectives mean for the majority of us? Are they even relevant in our lives, or merely the source for titillating news stories or fodder for futuristic crime movies? Do we consult these people via telephone chargelines, or at fairgrounds for fun, or because we have an inkling that maybe they can tell us what will be around the corner in our lives?

As creative, intelligent people we find the existence of forces we don't understand, fascinating. The sudden growth of interest in all things paranormal, particularly the "new-age," more spiritual side of ourselves that we are told we can reach with the aid of self-help books on the subject, is testament to our search for something more meaningful than the materialistic life we have developed.

It could be as the skeptics say, that ESP, psychic power, and the related phenomena, are all hocus-pocus; that we are hankering back to an age of superstition and witchcraft, rather than the rationality we spent centuries trying to achieve. It also could be that we are on the edge of some world-shattering discoveries that could change our whole understanding of ourselves, and even our planet.

It seems logical, therefore, when faced with such a vast array of differing views, to remain open minded. Reality-altering discoveries such as the fact that the earth isn't flat, or that as a race we are descended from primates, weren't accepted overnight. The discovery of a sixth sense would be just as earth shattering. It can't be measured, but then again neither can "smell," and who is to say that when we describe something as being "red," we are all describing the exact, identical color?

The human brain is extraordinary. We know so little about how our complex relationship of thoughts, actions, emotions, and physical reactions are interlinked, that it undoubtedly deserves serious study. Research into whether ESP exists or not is only a small part of this, but a vital one. If governments of both the United States and the former Soviet Union believe they managed to prove "something," and big business has tried to harness a marketable source of ESP, then why aren't police forces all over the world rushing to sign up the talents of psychic detectives?

Despite all the seemingly impressive case histories and positive testimonies in this book, there has never been a case of a psychic being able to walk into a police station and hand a list of clues to the officer on the desk to the extent that a crime is solved on the spot. The nearest a talented psychic seems to get is "seeing" an impression of the crime, the scene, the victim, or the perpetrator. These visions are never 100 percent accurate.

Colin Wilson, noted British author and researcher, refers to "James's Law," from William James's idea that no example of the paranormal should ever be 100 percent convincing. Certainly, when a psychic gives a list of impressions on a case, even if the leads are specific enough to be useful to police, not all will be accurate. This was discovered in the 1979 Los Angeles Police Department (LAPD) tests of the usefulness of psychic ability, when a group of twelve psychics were asked their impressions of various crimes.

If a psychic is able to accurately see the details of a crime, wouldn't he or she be able to stop it happening in the first place? Chris Robinson, the British dream detective, tries to do just that. But he has experienced the frustration of only being able to prove his accuracy rating by giving the authorities details of his dreams

LEFT: Noreen Renier's down-to-earth approach to matters psychic is now being adapted for FBI trainees in her own lecture presentations.

BELOW: FBI recruits, who could now be taking courses on "intuition" in order to "expand their thinking as police officers," according to Bureau chiefs.

ABOVE: John Hinckley's assassination attempt on President Reagan was predicted by Renier during one of her visits to the FBI, two months' prior to the incident.

and then having to sit back and watch the events unfold on his television.

Other psychics say they tune into the grief or pain of a victim, but it is only after something has happened that they are actually able to do this. Certainly, a psychic may be able to track a missing person or object, but the initial kidnap or burglary has to happen first. Noreen Renier, an American psychic who has lectured to the FBI on intuitive training, said in a 1993 interview with *Fate* magazine, "I do not solve crimes—the police do. I am an aid or investigative tool for the police. By picking up images and feelings that the average person cannot experience, I provide clues, new information, and perhaps a different angle to an unsolved crime."

Training those in the know

Nancy Myer, an American psychic who has been invited to lecture police officers on honing their own "psychic" instincts, also believes the powers simply don't work like people expect them to. She believes the police would have much better results if they themselves tried to use and develop their own psychic ability. Myer offers meditation courses, which she says are the best way to train the mind to listen to its psychic side. Even so, she believes a psychic can and often does get clues wrong, because "being psychic is a thought process that is difficult to control and direct."

Myer is very honest about her psychic power and the contribution it can make to a case. She told journalist Phyllis Galde, "I am not going to come up with the social security number or the license plate number of an assailant, or his name and address. Very few psychics have ever produced that type of information. I give a physical and psychological profile that is very accurate, including details about how the assailant connected with the victim ... A good psychic working on a police case should provide new information that can be researched and confirmed."

There have been cases, however, when the psychic's information has been considered extremely accurate by the police—so accurate, in fact, that the psychic has become a suspect in the crime. How else could they know so much detail?

When information is just too good

In 1980, Etta Louise Smith, a thirty-nine-year-old mother of three, had a vision about a murder. Presumably it disturbed her so much she felt compelled to go to the police with her thoughts. She claimed to have "seen" the murder of a young woman, she believed she knew the area where it had taken place, and gave lots of details about the attack leading up to the death. The LAPD were understandably intrigued. Unbeknown to Smith, however, her psychic sense had just described a murder that had taken place the night before. Melanie Urbibe, a nurse, had been raped and killed and her body dumped where Smith said it would be found.

Smith was then arrested on the charge of murder. Her detailed knowledge of the crime was so uncannily accurate, that to the investigating officer there could not have been any other explanation than that she had been party to the despicable act. Smith was locked up for four days before the real perpetrators were apprehended. Claiming she had suffered an emotional trauma from being treated as a murder suspect and incarcerated, Smith sued. In 1987, the

RIGHT: Intriguingly, both the FBI and the CIA take psi powers very seriously—so what could the future hold?

Psychic Horseplay

An intriguing case of psychic detective work, which takes the whole subject of ESP into further realms of discussion, is a 1952 case of a missing boy. Cited in Joe Nickell's book Psychic Sleuths, the psychic detective in this case wasn't human, but was, in fact, an American horse. Lady Wonder, the horse, was trained to answer questions through spelling out answers by pointing to letters painted on blocks. She was said to have special powers, and was certainly famous in her day.

When she was asked where the boy was, according to the tale, she spelled out "Pittsfield Water Wheel," which the police reinterpreted as "Field and Wilde's water pit," the name of an old, unused quarry, where the boy's body was eventually found.

Without getting into a discussion of animals and ESP, an area many people believe has just as much validity as human psychic ability, is the Lady Wonder case a fine example of how gullible we all can be if we really want to believe? Then again, just maybe?

mother who initially tried to help the police with a troubling psychic vision, was awarded just over $24,000 compensation.

Legal cases involving psychics always cause controversy. One of the most extraordinary examples was a libel case in 1986 when psychic Noreen Renier sued writer John Merrell, who had called her a fake. Although Renier lectured at the FBI Academy in Quantico, Virginia, in 1981, and says she has worked on "over 400 unsolved cases with city, county, and state law enforcement agencies in 38 states and five foreign countries," Merrell wasn't convinced by her psychic ability. The jury was, however, especially after two FBI officers testified Renier had helped them, or at least demonstrated she did possess an unusual ability to predict events or solve crimes. Renier was awarded a fee, but in the terms of the settlement she is not allowed to disclose the amount.

A $986,000 award was made to psychic Judith Richardson Haimes in 1986 in Philadelphia. She had allegedly been suffering from headaches when she tried to tune into her psychic powers, since receiving a computerized axial tomography (CAT) scan of her brain ten years previously. The money, which Lyons and Truzzi, authors of *The Blue Sense*, say is indicative of the public's growing acceptance of ESP and paranormal phenomena generally, was later withdrawn by the judge who said the jury had ignored his instructions.

So what do we make of all this evidence? On the one hand, certain police departments, and specifically individual officers, are convinced a talented psychic

BELOW: The campus of the FBI Training Academy at Quantico, Virginia, where Noreen Renier lectured in 1981. She believes that police can benefit from honing their own psychic skills.

ABOVE: Judith Richardson Haimes, who sued for medical malpractice after a CAT scan allegedly damaged her psychic powers.

RIGHT: Haimes's story relates how her psychic abilities were "put on trial" by skeptics, before she could claim compensation.

If these so-called psychic sleuths are deluding others as well as themselves, then the damage they can cause by wrongly identifying a child as dead, for example, is immeasurable. Undoubtedly, there are well-meaning people who aren't psychic at all, but who feel compelled to contact the police when they think they have somehow deciphered the clues to a crime reported on TV. The police are generally more than patient with this type of information, filing it "just in case" and thanking those who have contacted them.

The problem really lies with whether there is such a thing as a "sixth sense," which a few of us have developed or nurtured to a point that we can gain an insight into the past, present, and future, in a way that isn't detectable with our other five senses. Trying to prove one way or another whether this sixth

BELOW: Illusionist James Randi has become well known as a debunker of psychic claims.

can be of benefit in difficult cases; yet, on the other, skeptics argue psychics not only waste police resources, but cause unnecessary heartache as well.

Enter the skeptics

Psychic Sleuths: ESP and Sensational Cases, edited by Joe Nickell, contains several pages of black-and-white photographs. One of these pages depicts two freeze-frame shots of the American *Geraldo* TV show. The "star" guest is psychic Greta Alexander, who is holding the hand of a woman appealing for information about her missing son. The second frame in the sequence shows the woman's absolute look of shock, disbelief, and horror as the psychic detective says the boy is dead. The photo plate, with its two black-and-white frames, brings the whole subject back to reality with a heart-wrenching bump.

U.S. Psi Squad

ABOVE: Beverly Jaegers believes we all have innate intuitive abilities, which can be developed through practice.

Beverly Jaegers is a licensed private investigator who now runs the U.S. Psi Squad, a group offering training as well as help from its team members to police forces who request advice about unsolved crimes.

Jaegers founded the group in 1971 when she selected a team of her "psychic" students and they decided to try their hands at "a real puzzle." The case they chose was that of a missing woman named Sally Lucas; it was already five weeks' old. In a series of remote-viewing sessions, where psychometry was also used on some of the woman's possessions, it seems Jaegers and Jim Mueller, one of her senior students, managed to receive information about the crime that had taken place and where the woman's body would be found.

Although the team didn't actually find the body (a couple walking their dog had that misfortune) their descriptions were accurate enough for the case to be featured on television and in newspapers. It was decided their input had been useful enough that the team should try again. Psi Squad was formed. The team only works with police forces and other law enforcement agencies after they are directly approached, because media interest led to such a flood of cases that the group couldn't possibly deal with them all.

According to the publicity literature, the second case the Psi Squad tackled was "the kidnapping of a young girl … submitted to the [newly formed] Squad by 3rd District St. Louis Police. The group did not feel Jannae Collins had been kidnapped, and declared that she was well, had run away, was in California, and saw an Air Force uniform on an individual associated with her. About two weeks later, Jannae was eventually located in California, alive and well, and had been staying near an Air Force base and had been friendly with some of the airmen stationed there."

RIGHT AND BELOW: A remote-view sketch drawn by a Psi Squad member tallies with the location where a missing man was discovered in March 1997.

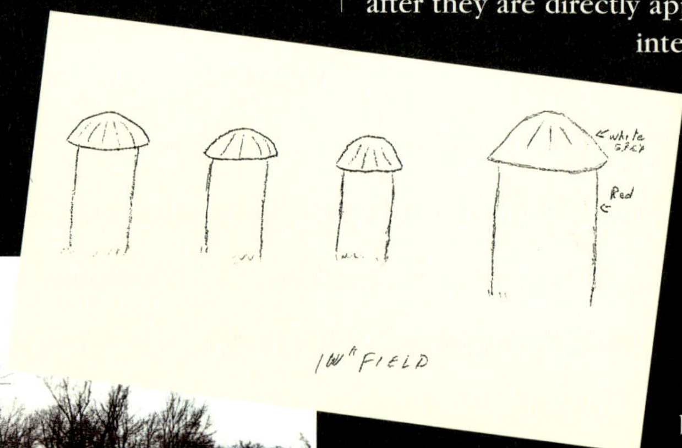

LEFT: *Jaegers (center) surrounded by members of the Psi Squad. Half the current squad are active police officers and ex-cops, and all recruits have trained psychic skills.*

The group say they worked on a "multiplicity of cases" through the 1970s, "ranging from homicide to a missing Picasso painting and a young black leopard from the St. Louis Zoo." They didn't seek publicity and say they prefer to work in confidence. Some of their work was also for an unnamed government agency.

The group was disbanded in 1983, but reformed with a slightly different focus, nine years later. Although the previous team had been credited with (again from Psi Squad literature) "locating the bodies of half a dozen missing persons, 'profiling' of murderers and victims, and location of several downed airplanes for Alaska's Civil Air Patrol, as well as conviction of murderers in several cases, including one in Kennett, Montana, and a serial killer in Belleville, Illinois. High profile cases involved a kidnapped busload of schoolchildren, the Ted Bundy case, and several cases of serial murder."

The new team was made up from members who not only had a trained psychic talent, but who also had some link with the legal profession, and preferably were police officers. Jaegers believes psi can be developed and nurtured in all of us. She doesn't allow Spiritualists—those who believe their extrasensory knowledge is given to them by the spirits of the dead—to become involved with the Psi Squad.

The team is still actively recruiting and says "all individuals with police background or law enforcement specialties will be considered." It doesn't charge for its work with police, considering what it does to be a "public service," and is currently developing a training program to be used with police forces, responding to the considerable interest from the authorities in the work it does. Recent psychic successes allegedly include locating a missing airplane in a California desert, providing "expert profiles of several murderers, including the physical description and name of the Sacramento Thrill Killer, and currently working on official homicide cases."

The group doesn't just offer the public its psychic detective services, though. It is concentrating more and more on the areas of psychic archaeology (reconstructing history, or locating historical artifacts using psychic ability) and business predictions. In the modern world, it seems this may be the way forward for the professional psychic, and it is certainly where the money is.

Jaegers has been linked to some extremely successful share dealings. In 1975, she helped J. P. Dixon, a man who had seen Jaegers on television discussing her detective work and then approached her about assisting with his business idea. It was the first time Jaegers was involved with dealings on Wall Street, but according to Psi Squad history, she accurately predicted Dixon would make a lot of money from buying coffee futures contracts. It took a while for the predictions to come true, but Dixon's futures became worth a fortune. So much so, he became a millionaire and gave Jaegers a substantial fee for helping him.

Since then, Jaegers has worked with all sorts of private clients, and even trained a few in how to remote view themselves. She was tested against three brokers and two other psychics by the *National Enquirer*, and she made the most money of all of them over a six-month period.

sense—ESP, psychic ability, or whatever—exists, is the key to the whole debate.

Is the ability to seemingly relive a violent crime to the point where the location of a body can be accurately pinpointed on a map, down to a mixture of gullible police and talented fraudsters? What are we to make of the fact that the United States government has admitted to funding and conducting years of research into ESP, especially now they have publicly stated it didn't achieve anything useful? All the information seems confusing, and scientifically verifiable facts are more than sparse.

Sony's psychic studies

Strangely enough, some interesting information that may throw light on the subject has come from an unexpected source. In 1997, a Japanese scientist gave a lecture to fellow colleagues at the sixteenth annual meeting of the Society for Scientific Exploration, at the University of Nevada. The talk was about research into paranormal phenomena, particularly ESP. What made the talk so extraordinary, was that Yoichiro Sako, the speaker, was a research director for the Sony Corporation, the massive electronics giant. Sony was pouring money into ESP research!

Surprisingly, the coverage of this groundbreaking news was limited if almost nonexistent: An article by Patrick Huyghe in issue 115 of *Fortean Times*; a mention in September 1996 *Wired* magazine; and an article on the Internet's Parascope page (http://www.parascope.com) called "The Sony Psi-Station", seem to be the best sources on the story. Yet, if Sony funded ESP research, they weren't doing it for public-interest purposes—they would have been evaluating whether there was any commercial potential or not.

In July 1998, there was more incredible news. The seven-year research program led by Sako was being shut down, despite Sony admitting they had proved ESP exists. It seems they couldn't find a commercial use for their discoveries, as D. Trull explains in Parascope, "they couldn't figure a way to make a buck out of it."

Yet, the research is significant. Sako had seemingly near-perfect results to share with his fellow scientists. In testing clairvoyance, which he did by getting his subjects to "remote view a crumpled piece of paper and redraw what they sensed was on it," Sako claimed a 97.1 percent success rate. That is, if accurate, a phenomenal score.

Writer Patrick Huyghe speculates there was more to the closure of the secretive paranormal department than Sony made public. He thinks the high-profile, hi-tech company is more than a little embarrassed it had to admit to studying the paranormal for seven years. The first rumblings of their research were really made public after the Aum cult gas attack in Tokyo in

ABOVE: Sony, the Japanese electronics giant, has admitted funding research into ESP.

LEFT: An Aum cult member. Fears over mind-control cults may be behind Sony's public statements.

1995 and the resulting murder trials, when the whole subject of mind control and the occult gripped the Japanese public. If the attack hadn't happened, would we know about the research?

So, officially we know that the U.S. government and one of the most-influential electronics firms in the world have both announced publicly they have invested considerable time and money in ESP research, and that they have found significant results. What are we to make, then, of their claims there is nothing they can do with the results? If the Japanese accuracy rating of 97.1 percent in tests of remote viewing are true, it seems the phenomenon can be replicated in laboratory conditions; it is demonstrable, and can be contained and defined.

Falling into the wrong minds

Although it is only speculation, it would not take a dedicated conspiracy theorist long to draw the conclusion that the CIA and Sony have chanced on something bigger than they dreamed of. And, if the U.S. government and a major corporation have managed to do it, then who knows who else has harnessed the power of the psychic?

This may sound, once again, as if we are wandering into Mulder and Scully territory, but Ingo Swann (see pages 95-6), the U.S.-government-trained remote viewer, issued a veiled warning to the West's governments in his response to the 1995 announcement that the American government would no longer be conducting research into remote viewing.

Swann voiced his fears in a paper published on the Internet in December 1995: "Several quite respectable sources have informed me that two major nations are making advances in psychoenergetics applications, one of which is remote viewing. It is also being alleged that a third smaller nation, with well known and advertised hatred of the American way of life, is also making progress. I believe those sources, because I know that liberated Russia sold for big bucks the Soviet psychic secrets three times over in order to acquire needed foreign exchange monies."

Are there secret laboratories hidden all over Eastern Europe where scientists are trying to capture ESP-related energy to power strange unknown spying devices? Who funds them if they do exist, governments

BELOW: A remote-staring experiment, where the subject pictured concentrates on a video image and tries to project it towards a "receiver" in another room.

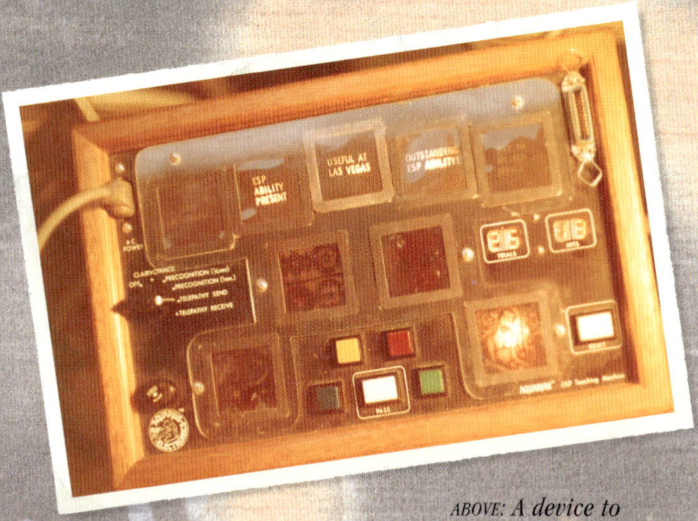

ABOVE: A device to measure ESP ability, designed by Russell Targ and Hal Puthoff at the Stanford Research Institute.

or organized crime? Certainly, new research coming out of Russia on the less controversial areas of psi-related research have alluded to interesting results. Feelings of pain have apparently been transmitted telepathically from starving rats on one floor of a research building to well-fed rats on a lower floor. The healthy rats showed all the symptoms of feeling the pain of starvation while having full bowls of food in front of them. Can pain or negative emotions be transferred from person to person as well?

Psychic cops vs. psi robbers

Can a talented psychic spy not only remote view documents, building plans, weapons installations, and eavesdrop on conversations, for example, but also actually affect targets to the point of driving them to suicide? It may be possible. Can the well-trained psychic spy commit the crimes their less ambitious counterparts are trying to solve?

What about the relationship between police forces and psychics? Certain forces and law firms have used psychics to help chose jury members in the United States, but they have also used psychologists and personality profilers. Psychic "evidence" is not admissible in court, and police officers have to be extremely careful they can prove by other means any clues or leads that have resulted from working with psychics.

There are, without doubt, charlatans who make big money out of allegedly being psychic. One only has to look at the numerous adverts for astrologers, mediums, and psychic healers in the back of everyday magazines to realize that claiming to have psychic powers can be big business.

One suggestion has been that the police, just like the American military did with its remote-viewing

BELOW: An FBI training session on how to deal with a hostage crisis. Remote viewers were supposedly successful in helping the U.S. government with several such situations.

program, should develop the psi ability of their recruits, thereby eliminating the need to contact outside psychics, and potentially increasing their solve-rate. The FBI have had lectures from psychics such as Noreen Renier, whose courses draw on techniques similar to those used by remote viewers, and also Kathryn Harwig, whose background is as an attorney and probation officer in Minneapolis.

Nurturing the "blue sense"

Harwig is a novelty because she has a conventional background, yet believes police benefit from ESP training. The police departments she works with think she has a point, too. According to an article, "ESPD Blue" by fellow remote viewer Stephan Schwartz, Harwig's course is offered to students at the University of Minnesota Police Department and "every station-house intake officer joining the St. Paul Police Department has taken [her] class."

ABOVE: Keith Charles, a British detective who also works as a medium, claims his psychic powers make him a better cop.

LEFT: Charles's unusual talents have led to many public appearances.

Schwartz says Harwig is accepted because of her legal background, and also because what she is teaching is not so far away from the norm that police officers can't see the benefits. Again, by teaching basic remote-viewing skills, Harwig aims to teach the police to develop their own intuition. She recommends her trainees take a few seconds to remote view a potentially difficult situation before plowing straight in. She believes this intuitive sense is increasingly necessary when officers have to be more culturally aware.

British Metropolitan Police CID Officer, Keith Charles, agrees with Harwig's belief that psychic powers can help an officer at work. In his book, cowritten with writer Derek Shuff and entitled *Psychic Cop: The Amazing Story of Britain's Only Clairvoyant Detective*, Charles talks about the benefits and problems of combining a career as a policeman and as a medium. Charles believes fervently in life after death, and his insight into the psychic side of life is relayed to him from the spirits.

Writing in his friendly, down-to-earth style, Charles says, "so now, by day, I am Detective Constable Keith Wright investigating and questioning the living. (Wright is my real name. My clairvoyant name is derived from Keith William Charles Wright.) Away from my police work, mostly at night, I am a medium who questions the dead. No wonder it confused my bosses." Charles even had to register his "outside interest" as a medium on police files because he earns money from his clairvoyant performances, so all his colleagues know about his unusual gift.

For a British police officer to be so frank about such a controversial area, especially as Charles believes his particular insight derives from the dead, is extremely surprising. Yet, his book is full of anecdotes about how his powers have helped people, from celebrities to members of the public he meets at his performances.

Although he is always very careful to use only official police procedures while at work, mindful that "spirit messages do not make good police evidence," Charles says, "I believe I am a better policeman by being psychic because I can bring another dimension into my work—my psychic eye often leads me in certain directions."

Good cop, great cop

Riley G., an ex-New York Police Department (NYPD) cop who now runs a private detective agency called Riley G. Enterprises (see pages 70–71 for a case study), also believes his psychic powers helped him in his career as a police officer. Riley G. retired because of injury after eleven-and-a-half years as a police officer. He worked for the U.S. Army military police as well as the NYPD, and says "while in both organizations the only one who had a clue about my abilities was my partner in the NYPD. During my time with the NYPD, I used my abilities to hunt down and arrest illegal gun carriers and drug dealers. At the time of my medical retirement from the NYPD, my partner and I had the number one arrest time in our precinct."

Riley G. says his "remote viewing and psychic sensing" skills were particularly useful to him when he was assigned to a Special Reaction Team, which dealt with terrorism against American personnel and bases in Europe. He doesn't do individual readings for people because he believes his talents are best used helping solve crimes. Although only working privately now, he recalled a case where both he and his former partner made an arrest in March 1989 "with more than a little help from my sixth sense." They were on a patrol in their police car when a premonition told Riley G. to check a white vehicle parked two blocks away. From where he was, around a corner, he couldn't even see a white vehicle, but as they turned, they saw the car.

The three people in the white car saw the police and sped off. Riley G. and his partner gave chase. The white car crashed and the occupants fled. Again,

ABOVE: The NYPD was home to psychic detective Riley G., who believes his sixth sense was essential to his police work on the streets of New York.

Detecting Life on Other Planets

An extraordinary book was published in 1997 by Dr. Courtney Brown, a professor of political science at Emory University, in Atlanta. Cosmic Voyage: A Scientific Discovery of Extraterrestrials Visiting Earth, caused a storm among Brown's colleagues because in it he describes exploring the cosmos and meeting with extraterrestrial entities through the means of remote viewing.

Brown says he was trained in remote viewing by a former member of the U.S. military remote-viewing program, although he doesn't reveal who exactly. Brown believes, as his book's title suggests, that he has scientific proof that at least two different races of aliens have visited earth, and that he has been meeting with entities from a sort of interplanetary government to forge the way for humans to one day mingle with them.

Taking psychic spying to the extreme, Brown says "the research presented in this book was conducted using rigorous and exacting remote-viewing protocols that were recently developed for the U.S. military for espionage purposes." The prologue describes the book as "a detailed examination of two societies of known intelligent extraterrestrial life. More specifically, this volume is the result of years of work observing alien cultures whose activities here on earth have been very pronounced." Brown believes he has psychically spied on, and then interacted with, both Martians and "Gray" aliens. He believes we as humans, have a close relationship with the two alien races.

Has Dr. Brown taken psychic spying way over the top? If his research is accurate (just so far ahead of its time that it is too much for the majority of us to comprehend), then he would have to deserve the title of "Psychic Detective Inspector," because he may have solved one of the biggest mysteries that has plagued mankind for centuries. Brown claims to have remote viewed into alien civilizations and believes if others try scientific remote viewing these alien entities, then they will confirm his findings.

Riley G. says he had a premonition that one of the people was armed. Sure enough the driver pointed a gun at the police car before running off. When they eventually apprehended the man and took him back to the police station, the suspect turned out to be wanted in connection with "numerous robberies, attempted murder, weapons possession, and countless related crimes. We had just arrested one of NYC's most wanted criminals. All this from a psychic feeling."

Riley G. Enterprises also conducts training sessions in positive thinking and self-hypnosis techniques for corporations wanting their staff to benefit from developing their own inner strength. His is not the only private company in the ESP world. If government departments are wary of being associated with paranormal activities, then it seems the public is a little more accepting than they think. ESP ability is being packaged and marketed on a grand scale, not least with numerous self-help books, tapes, and videos, teaching everything from out-of-body experiences to divining the future with a crystal ball!

Various companies and groups are offering their psychic services to big business or interested individuals. In an arena where graphology (the study of handwriting) was once considered "paranormal," but is now commonly used as a personality-testing tool, other out-of-the-ordinary skills are being utilized.

There are those at the more lighthearted end of the spectrum, such as the U.S.-based Hillhouse Investigations: Psychic Detective Agency (http://www.psychicdetectives.com/main.htm), "We, the members of Hillhouse Investigations, Inc., have a mission: To provide you, the man or woman on the street with a dependable variety of solutions to your paranormal difficulties. If you have ever lost sleep because of those unexplainable 'bumps' in the night ..." The agency says all their "psychic predictions are accomplished through the use of Official Hillhouse Mystic Crystals," just in case you were wondering.

On a more serious note, Angela Thompson Smith, author of *Remote Perceptions: Out-of-Body Experiences, Remote Viewing, and Other Normal Abilities*, writes "There are at least four groups around the continental United States that are attempting to put remote viewing onto a practical, business basis. These groups solicit private clients, in industry and commerce, and in government, to carry out disciplined technical remote viewing."

One of the companies she is referring to is P>S>I Tech, staffed by some of the ex-military remote viewers under Lyn Buchanan (see page 94). Paul Smith, another Fort Meade remote viewer along with Ingo Swann and Pat Price, has set up a training program called Remote Viewing Instructional Service, and Angela Thompson Smith herself, runs a "nonprofit organization called the Inner Vision Institute, to teach extended remote

LEFT: Angela Thompson Smith remote-viewed the Unabomber before his eventual capture.

BELOW: There are fears that psychic skills could be harnessed by organized crime syndicates.

If ESP Exists, Can Anyone Do It?

While it would be silly to suggest anyone should suddenly besiege their local police station with pages of notes of their dreams, or conversations they have had with their aunt who has been dead for twenty years, there is no reason why we as individuals shouldn't try to be more in tune with whatever our "sixth sense" is. If it doesn't exist as the skeptics claim, then we are fooling no-one but ourselves.

Developing the psychic detective in yourself is, apparently, fairly simple. Although there are courses to take, mostly in America, they can be expensive. Home study courses are often costly, too, requiring the individual to purchase more videos and written material as they progress through the stages.

For the curious student wanting to learn how to divine answers to life's problems for themselves or their family and friends, there are some excellent divination books available which teach a whole range of techniques from tarot cards and rune stones,

RIGHT: A true psychic interpretation of the tarot relies on the reader trusting their own sixth sense.

BELOW: The mystical symbols of the rune stones require intense study before they can be used as psychic inspiration.

"The basis for developing any psychic ability is being able to block out unwanted outside forces or interferences, and concentration on a specific thought, area, or problem."

through to crystal and color therapy. At the very least, they can provide an interesting hobby and a good talking point among friends. Even professional psychics who consult the cards about their client's fortunes, have the sense to realize they are only a tool for focusing the thoughts of that person. If we are told to expect good fortune, or that we are about to meet the partner of our dreams, then on this basic level, using divination to become more positive and channeled in life, can't be a bad thing.

Natural intuition, which we are all said to possess, is also supposed to be easy to nurture. Most teachers of ESP and remote-viewing techniques concentrate on meditative procedures to relax the subject and allow them to focus the mind on a specific problem or target. While the majority of us have no need of remote-viewing skills—even if they do accurately portray what is happening somewhere in a given time-frame—the pace of Western life means most of us *would* probably benefit from slowing down and contemplating life now and again.

The basis for developing any psychic ability is being able to block out unwanted outside forces or interferences, and concentration on a specific thought, area, or problem. The power of positive thought isn't just the stuff of new-age gurus. Even conventional medical doctors now recognize a body is likely to heal quicker if the patient's mind believes they are going to get better. The same techniques can be applied to all areas of our lives.

The use of divination tools to help consolidate our judgment should not be taken too seriously. They may well help to focus on a particular area of our lives, but their supposed message is open to many different interpretations, just like our daily horoscopes.

A simple way to test your own intuitive powers, is to see how many times you can correctly guess the flipping of a coin. The probability of getting it right is fifty percent. Any more than that, and maybe you have a talent worth investigating.

If you are interested in developing your intuitive mind, or would simply like to carry out more research in this area, approach some of the organizations listed at the end of this book.

LEFT: Meditation is the key to developing mindpower and focusing on your intuitive side.

viewing." These companies run training programs, which they have based to a greater or lesser degree on the techniques discovered by government-sponsored research into remote viewing.

As for practical applications, Thompson Smith has some good ideas for the future of remote viewing, speculating it might be a useful skill to develop for visually impaired or physically disabled people. Remote viewing would also be useful for business: trouble-shooters could solve internal management problems psychically, complex machinery or technology could be serviced using "remote reviewing" which would be safer and more cost effective, memos could be sent telepathically—the list is endless.

Dowsing: The modern detective work

The future of psychic detection seems to be hovering between covert uses, particularly linked to espionage or crime, or overt uses by private companies promoting remote viewing, or sixth-sense abilities, for the good—or at least financial gain—of individuals.

Uri Geller is a rich man, a fact which has probably been at the root of many of the attacks on his character. He made most of his money, according to his various books and interviews, by helping private companies find oil, minerals, and gold. He did this using his psychic powers—he is an accomplished dowser.

Geller combines his own psychic talents with more conventional ones in the form of his business associates who have worked in the mining industry. Calling the team Uri Geller Associates, they offer services, which include locating specific areas where valuable mineral deposits are likely to be found.

In the 1980s, the team was hired by Zanex Limited, an Australian company, which wanted to locate a potential source of diamonds in the Solomon Islands. Geller's website quotes the director of Zanex giving a glowing report of the psychic's detective work, saying he'd "never drill an oil well without asking Uri Geller's advice first."

The practice of dowsing has been well documented, if not universally accepted, and some of its properties are useful in helping explain other psychic detection tools, such as psychometry. British archaeologist Tom Lethbridge was intrigued by the reactions of a forked hazel twig over volcanic rock in the early 1930s, and decided to research whether it had been fluke or whether his simple device could actually help find various objects, and possibly detect what the objects were.

Although this sounds far-fetched, Lethbridge carried out extensive tests using a pendulum, and believed he had discovered something very exciting. Depending on what substance was lying beneath the pendulum, the dowsing device would react only when the string was held at a specified length. Although a surprisingly simple method, Lethbridge

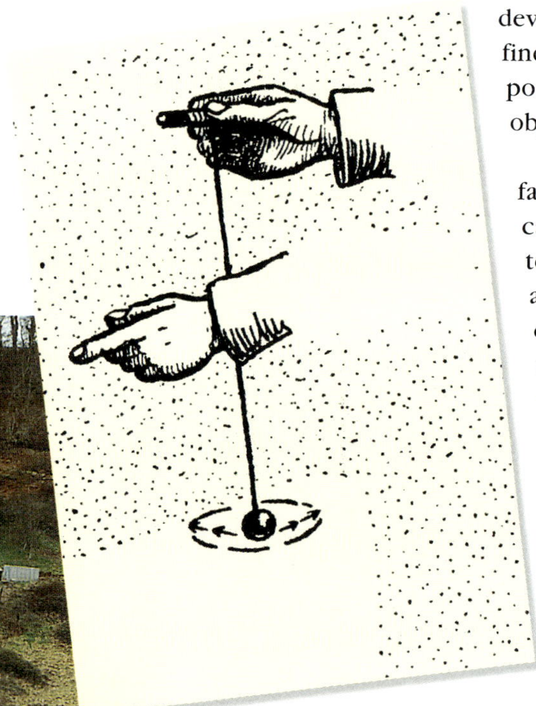

ABOVE: Tom Lethbridge made the fascinating discovery that the dowsing pendulum only reacts at a certain length, depending on the properties of what lies underneath the device.

LEFT: Hole Mill in Devon, England, where Lethbridge experimented with dowsing in his own garden, excavating archaeological finds including pots dating from Tudor times.

ABOVE: American soldiers uncover a Viet Cong tunnel during the war in Vietnam. The U.S. military often relied on the ancient art of dowsing to pinpoint the location of the tunnels.

achieved considerable results—the pendulum would react, for instance, over silver when the string was exactly twenty-two inches long. Not only that, but the pendulum would be still until the string reached that length, time and time again. Soon Lethbridge realized the number of circular movements the actual pendulum made while being held over an object, was just as significant as the length of the string.

Testing and retesting endless metals, objects, plants, and animals, gave Lethbridge a long list of "values" at which the pendulum would gyrate, and his results could be repeated time and time again. Additional research revealed the pendulum also seemed to respond to emotions. At forty inches the pendulum could detect anger; he also speculated that it would respond to concepts as well.

Lethbridge's work has considerable bearing on explaining how psychic detectives can locate missing bodies by dowsing over a map, or how they can pinpoint murder scenes or hideouts. If the pendulum can pick up emotions, and all the psychic detectives interviewed agree they are better at detecting emotive crimes, then it would be easy to pick up an extremely violent or fear-related site. Also, the theory goes some way to explaining how, when a psychic detective visits a crime scene or is given objects belonging to suspects or victims, they manage to pick up impressions of what has happened.

Lethbridge's list of values, and his alleged discovery that emotions are somehow recorded by our surroundings, was an important body of work. It led him to believe that, according to an article entitled "Gateway to Other Worlds," published in the now-out-of-print *Unexplained* magazine, "nature generates fields of static electricity in certain places, particularly near running water". These "fields are capable of picking up and recording the thoughts and feelings of human beings and other living creatures." Because we as individuals are also surrounded by a field of static electricity, it may be possible that energy can be transferred, which is why we may pick up feelings of sadness or anger in certain places. Equally so, Lethbridge hypothesized, we could transfer our emotions onto a physical place.

The psychic future

If dowsing can be put to good use with cost-effective and accurate results by gas, water, and mineral exploration companies, would the police find it easier to employ someone who called themselves a dowser rather than a psychic? Certainly, the U.S. military has not had any problem admitting it used dowsing techniques to locate mines and Viet Cong tunneling systems during the war in Vietnam.

As more and more of the techniques and powers used by psychic detectives are being explained, or at least investigated by recognized bodies, somehow they don't seem so paranormal. Their "sixth sense" becomes less the stuff of *The X Files* and more a very real possibility. The world of ESP and the linked phenomena that the psychic detective employs is most definitely not an exact science, because if it were, it would be very difficult for any crime to be committed. But there is most certainly a starting point here which deserves and needs much more research. What is clear though, is that the world of the psychic detective is a fascinating one, and one which could be the key we need to answering some of life's most important questions.

Resources

For those interested in further research in the area of psychic studies, the organizations listed below may be useful.

The Society for Psychical Research promotes and supports serious scientific study of psychic and paranormal occurrences. It publishes a quarterly journal, has an extensive library, and invites membership from interested members of the public.
49 Marloes Road, Kensington,
London W8 6LA, U.K.

The American Society for Psychical Research promotes similar research to its UK counterpart above, and also produces its own literature.
5 West 73rd Street, New York,
NY 10023, U.S.A.

The Center for Scientific Anomalies Research are always interested to hear about cases involving alleged psychic abilities.
P.O. Box 1052, Ann Arbor, MI 48103, U.S.A.

The Rhine Research Center is a nonprofit research and education organization dedicated to the study of parapsychology.
1215 S. Kihei Road, #433, P.O. Box 959,
Kihei, Hawaii 96753-0959, U.S.A.

Superpowers of the Human Biomind is Ingo Swann's Internet resource which publishes many of his writings and articles, as well as a thorough history of the U.S. government's remote-viewing program, and has excellent links to related sites and papers.
http://www.biomindsuperpowers.com/Pages/Superpowers.html

Controlled Remote Viewing is the homepage of Lynn Buchanan, an ex-U.S. government remote viewer whose P>S>I Internet site and company are mentioned in Chapter Four. The site contains comprehensive explanations, links, and articles.
http://www.crviewer.com/
37 Camino Ranchitos, Alamogordo,
NM 88310, U.S.A.

Inner Vision is the remote-viewing training company founded by author Angela Thompson Smith.
http://www.ivri.com/

Firedocs is an excellent Internet resource for those who want more in-depth information about remote viewing, as the site says, it has "way more remote viewing info than you'll have the time to read."
http://www.firedocs.com/remoteviewing/core2.html

Paranormal Management Systems, the company run by U.K. remote viewer Tim Rifat, has online information about the company and the history of remote viewing.
http://www.fastnet.co.uk/pms/info.html
P.O. Box 2749, Brighton BN2 2DR, U.K.

There are numerous books available for developing your own "intuitive" abilities. A selection of titles for enthusiastic beginners is listed below, but it is certainly worth visiting larger bookstores, libraries, or even exploring on the Internet to find more information.

SPECIFIC DIVINATION METHODS

The Power of the Pendulum,
T. C. Lethbridge, Arkana (now out of print but well worth trying to track down)

The Elements of Pendulum Dowsing,
Tom Graves, Element, 1997

Dowsing: Ancient Origins and Modern Uses,
Rodney Davies, Thorsons, 1997

The Pendulum Kit,
Sig Lonegren, Simon and Schuster, 1990

Tarot Made Easy,
Nancy Garen, Fireside, 1989

The Mythic Tarot Workbook,
Juliet Sharman-Burke and Liz Greene, Rider, 1988

The Dream Book: Symbols for Self-Understanding,
Betty Bethards, Element, 1997

Using the Runes: A Comprehensive Introduction to the Art of Runecraft,
D. Jason Cooper, Thorsons, 1997

Palmistry Made Practical,
Elizabeth Daniels Squire, Wilshire Book Company, 1978

PSYCHIC AWARENESS

Psychic Empowerment,
Joe H. Slate Ph.D., Llewellyn, 1995

Psychic Protection: Creating Positive Energies for People and Places,
William Bloom, Piatkus, 1997

Intuition Workout: A Practical Guide to Discovering and Developing Your Inner Knowing,
Nancy Rosanoff, Aslan Publishing, 1991

The Psychic Workbook: Discover and Enhance Your Hidden Psychic Powers,
Craig Hamilton-Parker, Vermillion, 1995

As I See It: A Psychic's Guide to Developing Your Sensing and Healing Abilities,
Betty F. Balcome, Piatkus, 1997

Psychic Development for Beginners: An Easy Guide to Releasing and Developing Your Psychic Abilities,
William Hewitt, Llewellyn, 1996

Are You Psychic?: Unlocking the Power Within,
Dr. Hans Holzer, Avery Publishing Group, 1997

Coming Out of Your Psychic Closet: How to Unlock Your Naturally Intuitive Self,
Lynn B. Robinson, Factor Press, 1994

Development of Psychic Powers,
Melita Denning and Osborne Phillips, Llewellyn, 1987

TESTING YOUR PSYCHIC ABILITY BY COMPUTER

Alan Vaughan, Ph.D., is a prolific author, researcher and also a psychic. He has worked with SRI International and the Mobius Society and has been described as an "international authority on psi." With fellow researcher Jack Houck, he has developed a PC software program called Psychic Reward, which is publicized as "the first scientifically proven system for training your intuitive powers." Billed as being able to increase the ability to "sense the future," Psychic Reward aims to encourage thinking based on intuitive responses rather than logic.

The software is available from http://www.alanvaughan.com/psychicreward.html

Bibliography

Bird, Christopher, The Divining Hand: The 500-Year-Old Mystery of Dowsing, Whitford Press, 1993

Brookesmith, Peter (ed.), Cult and Occult: The Unexplained File (previously published in partworks as The Unexplained), BCA, 1985

Charles, Keith and Shuff, Derek, Psychic Cop, Blake, 1995

Donkin, André, Dead Giveaways, Element, 1998

Evans, Hilary (ed.), Frontiers of Reality: Where Science Meets the Paranormal, BCA, 1991

Eysenck, Hans J. and Sargent, Carl, Explaining the Unexplained: Mysteries of the Paranormal, Prion, 1993

Geller, Uri and Lyon Playfair, Guy, The Geller Effect, Grafton, 1988

Karcher, Stephen, The Illustrated Encyclopedia of Divination, Element, 1997

Kurtz, Paul (ed.), A Skeptic's Handbook of Parapsychology, Prometheus Books, 1985

Lyons, Arthur and Truzzi, Marcello, The Blue Sense: Psychic Detectives and Crime, Mysterious Press, 1991

Matthews, John (ed.), The World Atlas of Divination, Tiger, 1998

Nicholas, Margaret, The World's Greatest Psychics and Mystics, Hamlyn, 1994

Nickell, Joe (ed.), Psychic Sleuths: ESP and Sensational Cases, Prometheus Books, 1994

Ostrander, Sheila and Schroeder, Lynn, Psychic Discoveries: Behind the Iron Curtain, Bantam Books, 1970

Ostrander, Sheila and Schroeder, Lynn, Psychic Discoveries: The Iron Curtain Lifted, Souvenir Press, 1997

Robinson, Chris and Boot, Andy, Dream Detective, Warner Books, 1997

Stokes, Doris, Voices in my Ear, Aiden Ellis, 1980

Thompson Smith, Angela, Remote Perceptions: Out-of-Body Experiences, Remote Viewing and Other Normal Abilities, Hampton Roads, 1998

various authors, Mysteries of the Unexplained, Reader's Digest Association, 1982

various authors, The World of the Paranormal: A Unique Insight into the Unexplained (previously published in partworks as The Unexplained), Orbis, 1998

various authors, The X Files: Enigmas of Mind, Space and Time (previously published in partworks as The Unexplained), Index, 1995

Wilson, Colin (ed.), The Directory of Possibilities, Webb and Bower, 1981

Wilson, Colin, The Psychic Detectives: Paranormal Crime Detection, Telepathy and Psychic Archeology, Mercury House, 1985

Index

Acknowledgments

I would like to thank everyone who has helped with the research for this book and apologize if I haven't mentioned you by name. As with any book of this nature, much research and background information relies on the work of previous investigators and authors, all of whom I have done my best to credit in full. Particular thanks must go to: Marcello Truzzi whose help with research articles and recommended reading was invaluable; author Colin Wilson for his generosity; k.t. Frankovich and her husband David Taub; Riley G.; Nancy Myer; Noreen Renier; Lyn Guest de Swarte and everyone at Psychic News; Janet Bord at the Fortean Picture Library. I would also like to thank Uri Geller who first got me interested in the subject of psychic detection. Many thanks to Sue Evins for being a friend as well as an excellent project editor, and of course to family and friends who have to put up with my deadlines—most of all Ian and our new little family.

Picture Credits

KEY: b = bottom; c = center; i = inset; l = left; r = right; t = top.

Greta Alexander: 52.
Dorothy Allison: 42t, 44b, 45, 46.
Corbis: 80, 81, 91tl.
Fortean Picture Library: 13b, 28b, 33c, 34tr, 73br, 88br, 89tl, 93br, 94bl, 95b, 97b, 109, 111.
Frank Spooner Pictures: 18b, 60, 63, 73tl, 85br, 89br, 92, 102b, 104b.
k.t. Frankovich: 74.
Judith Richardson Haimes: 105tl, 105c.
The Hulton Getty Collection: 50.
The Image Bank: 35tli.
Beverly Jaegers: 106, 107.
The Kobal Collection: 93tr.
The London Dungeon: 16.
Mary Evans Picture Library: 12, 22, 24/25, 26bl, 28tr, 29, 32b, 47, 96tc.
Nancy Myer: 78, 79.
via Orbis Publishing: 13t Henry Gris, 48tr John Frost, 48c Psychic News, 110tl Elmar Gruber, 116 Roger Mayne.
Sheila Ostrander: 56.
Penguin Books: 98tc.
Popperfoto: 6/7, 14c, 19tl, 21br, 23, 27, 30, 32tl, 33t, 35tl, 36, 38br, 40, 41tr, 43cr, 44tr, 64tl, 76tr, 84c, 86/87, 87, 90, 98tr, 103tl. 108c, 110b, 113c.
Quadrillion Publishing: 26tr, 34b, 51, 55, 59, 114.
Noreen Renier: 66, 67, 102cr.
Rex Features: 15b, 18bl, 20, 49tr, 53tl, 57, 58, 64tr, 69br, 72, 75, 76tl, 76br, 94tr, 99, 104tr, 105br, 112bl, 113br.
Tim Rifat: 88c.
Riley G: 35br, 70, 71.
The Ronald Grant Archive: 54bl.
Science Photo Library: 31br, 53b, 62, 68, 100, 112tr, 115.
Topham Picturepoint: 14br, 15tl, 19tr, 21cl, 25tr, 31tl, 38bl, 39, 41tl, 42bl, 43t, 49b, 65, 77, 84b, 91b, 95c, 96cb, 98tl, 103br.
TRH Pictures: 97t, 117.
Ubiquity: 108tr.

JACKET ILLUSTRATIONS

Front cover: Science Photo Library (cr); The Image Bank (cl).
Back cover: Fortean Picture Library (tr); Frank Spooner Pictures (tl).

Note: In sourcing the photographs for this book, every reasonable effort has been made by the publisher to contact the original copyright holder and obtain permission in writing for the use of the photographs.